Feasting with the Father

A 40-Day Devotional Journey to the Lord's Table

JULY 23, 2025

VICTORY LIFE MINISTRIES

261 Cove Road, Tazewell, Va 24651

Feasting with the Father

Aaron Roberts

Published by Victory Life Ministries, 2025.

Table of Contents

Epigraph

"And it shall come to pass, that every one that is left of all the nations... shall even go up from year to year to worship the King, the Lord of hosts, and to keep the feast..."

— Zechariah 14:16, KJV

"Blessed is he that shall eat bread in the kingdom of God."

— Luke 14:15, KJV

"Thou preparest a table before me in the presence of mine enemies: thou anointest my head with oil; my cup runneth over."

— Psalm 23:5, KJV

"Gather My saints together unto Me; those that have made a covenant with Me by sacrifice."

— Psalm 50:5, KJV

"And He took bread, and gave thanks, and brake it, and gave unto them, saying, This is My body which is given for you: this do in remembrance of Me."

— Luke 22:19, KJV

"To him that overcometh will I grant to sit with Me in My throne... I will come in to him, and will sup with him, and he with Me."

— Revelation 3:20–21, KJV

"Blessed are they which are called unto the marriage supper of the Lamb."

— Revelation 19:9, KJV

What if every altar in Scripture was meant to lead you to a table?

What if the fire of revival wasn't the end—but the beginning of deeper fellowship, covenant, and glory?

In the devotional, _Feasting with the Father_, start discovering the sacred pattern woven through every covenant from Genesis to Revelation: God calls His people to the altar, but He forms them at the table.

From the smoke of sacrifice to the bread of communion, this book leads you into the heart of God's presence—where lives are offered, love is shared, and revival becomes relationship.

The altar consumes what we surrender.

The table reveals Who we remember.

And both prepare us for the feast to come.

Whether you're a pastor, intercessor, worshiper, or simply hungry for more of God, this journey will stir your soul, deepen your understanding of covenant, and reignite your love for His presence. This book doesn't finish the journey - it begins it.

Come to the fire. Stay for the feast.

Revival starts at the altar—but it lives at the table.

"Blessed are those that shall eat bread in the kingdom of God" – from Luke 14:15

Feasting with the Father
A 40-Day Devotional Journey
to the Lord's Table

—◦◦◦—

**"A Sacred Journey from the Fire and Altar
to the Glory and Fellowship of the Table"**

Published by Victory Life Ministries
ISBN: 979-8-218-72870-0
First Printing: 2025
For permissions or inquiries, please contact: victorylifemissions@gmail.com

Dedication

I DEDICATE THIS SERIES of writing to my dear wonderful wife, Regina, my blessed children and grandchildren, my beloved parents, my two brothers, and my grandparents, and the wide spread of family and friends who have added to my life immeasurably – I have come to know the Lord better because of you.

——————— ⟨∾⟩ ———————

and last but not least - to all those who have sat with ●●●●● me and shared a meal of fellowship—thank you. May your memories be as lasting and rich as mine

Devotional Introduction

JULY 23, 2025

The Fire and the Table Series – A Journey of Revival and Glory.
This study was born in the fire of revival.

It began during a series of altar-centered meetings—gatherings where hungry hearts cried out for God's presence, and the Spirit moved with unmistakable power. The message that carried those meetings was titled *"A People for His Love: The Journey to Revival."* It awakened something deep—not just in those who came to the altar, but in me.

In one particular gathering, following prayer and small group reflection, I found myself lingering in the presence of God. As I opened the Scriptures again, a shocking revelation unfolded before my eyes: Wherever God formed covenant with His people—at the altar—it was always followed by a table. Every major covenant, from Genesis to Revelation, carried this sacred pattern. The altar... then the table. The fire... then the glory. Sacrifice... then fellowship.

That discovery gripped my spirit. The study became intense, alive, and deeply fulfilling. I found myself diving headfirst into the Word, tracing the divine design that wove its way through the garden of Eden, through Sinai, through the upper room, and into the marriage supper of the Lamb.

As I meditated further, it became clear—this wasn't just theological. It was personal. I realized that my own life had been formed by the table. Growing up in a small church nestled in the Appalachian Mountains. was shaped not only by the fire of altar calls, but by what came after: the potluck table, the communion bread, the sacred space of shared meals and holy conversations. I was discipled by the fellowship that followed the fire.

And in that moment, it was as if the Lord invited me: "Follow Me into the fire—and you will find the glory of My table."

This is a covenantal study. It is marked not only by sacrifice—our call to become living offerings upon His altar—but by the fellowship that follows: the peace offering, the bread of covenant, the wine of remembrance, the table of unity, and the place of rest.

There is a final table God has prepared for us all. And He is preparing us for that table.

For months, I was unsure whether to begin this work as a daily devotional or as a more theological exposition. I love studying the depths of Hebrew terms and the unfolding patterns of Scripture. But in prayer, I felt the Lord impress upon me a clear direction: make this simple. Serve it like a meal. Offer it in slow, small bites—truths that can marinate in the soul. "Let Me," the Lord seemed to say, "prepare My people for My table."

So here it is—a book about the altar and the table, the fire and the fellowship, the sacrifice and the glory. May it stir your heart toward revival. May it lead you back to the altar. But even more, may it teach you to abide at the table.

For the fire draws us near—but the table holds us there.

Let's journey together,

Aaron Roberts

Day 1 – Abraham's Covenant: A Meal of Promise

SCRIPTURE:

"**18** And the Lord appeared unto him in the plains of Mamre: and he sat in the tent door in the heat of the day; **2**And he lift up his eyes and looked, and, lo, three men stood by him: and when he saw them, he ran to meet them from the tent door...And I will fetch a morsel of bread... And they said, So do, as thou hast said. **6**And Abraham hastened into the tent **8**And he took butter, and milk, and the calf which he had dressed, and set it before them; and he stood by them under the tree, and they did eat." —Genesis 18:1–8 (KJV - selected)

Devotional Meditation

Under the hot sun of Mamre, Abraham wasn't just hosting strangers—he was setting a table for the Lord. In what looked like a simple act of hospitality, a holy moment unfolded: the divine entered Abraham's tent, received his offering, and confirmed the promise of a child in due season. The meal was not merely food—it was a table of communion, a table of covenant, a table of promise.

God often visits us not with fanfare, but with quiet footprints at the door of our lives. Abraham, tuned to faith and friendship with God, responded with immediate generosity. He ran to meet the visitors. He hurried to prepare the best. He served standing under the tree while they ate. And in the presence of that humble meal, the Lord reaffirmed His word: "At the appointed time I will return to you, and Sarah will have a son."

Every table we set for the Lord—every act of quiet worship, surrender, and hospitality—is an altar where promises are rekindled. Revival doesn't always start with fire from heaven; sometimes, it begins with bread, milk, and a willing heart. God is a God of covenant, and His covenant is often confirmed at a table.

Reflection

Are there "ordinary" moments in your life where God might be visiting?

What does it look like to make space for God's presence in your daily routine?

What promises of God feel delayed in your life—and how might the table of intimacy renew your faith to believe again?

Prayer: The Fire of Promise

O Lord of the Covenant,
    You appeared to Abraham not in thunder or earthquake,
but in the gentle form of three visitors under the shade of a tree.
Teach me to recognize You in the stillness, in the quiet places,
in the guests I serve and the moments I treasure.
As I set a table in my heart,

let it be a table of welcome for Your Word.
Revive the promises You've spoken over my life.
Awaken my spirit to run to You, to serve You,
and to believe that even now, at the appointed time,
You are bringing forth life.
I receive Your presence today with faith,
and I welcome Your promise to reignite hope in my soul.
Let this day be the beginning of my revival at the table.
In Jesus' name, Amen.

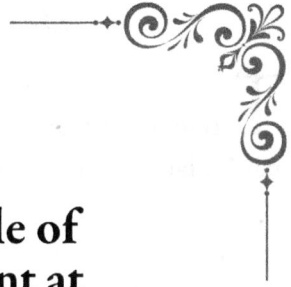

Day 2 – The Table of Jacob: A Covenant at Mizpah

SCRIPTURE:

"⁴⁹And Mizpah; for he said, The Lord watch between me and thee, when we are absent one from another. ⁵⁰If thou shalt afflict my daughters, or if thou shalt take other wives beside my daughters, no man is with us; see, God is witness betwixt me and thee. ⁵¹And Laban said to Jacob, Behold this heap, and behold this pillar, which I have cast betwixt me and thee: ⁵²This heap be witness, and this pillar be witness, that I will not pass over this heap to thee, and that thou shalt not pass over this heap and this pillar unto me, for harm. ⁵³The God of Abraham... judge betwixt us. ⁵⁴Then Jacob offered sacrifice upon the mount, and called his brethren to eat bread: and they did eat bread" —Genesis 31:44, 48–49 (KJV - selected)

Devotional Meditation

The Table at Mizpah was not a feast of abundance, it was a boundary marked by covenant. Jacob and Laban, after years of manipulation, conflict, and mistrust, came together to part in peace. A simple meal was shared on a heap of stones, and with it came a solemn agreement: "May the Lord watch between you and me when we are absent one from the other." God would be there to witness their relationship and covenant.

Though not born of deep friendship, this meal was saturated with the fear of the Lord. It marked a threshold. Jacob was finally leaving his old life behind—his labor under Laban, his running from Esau—and stepping forward toward the land of promise with a new identity. The table at Mizpah became the place where old wounds were released, where a broken relationship yielded to divine oversight, and where the future was entrusted to God.

Not every table is celebratory—some are tables of reconciliation. And even then, the bread broken and shared is still sacred. Mizpah reminds us that peace with others is part of our walk with God. Covenant is not merely about what we receive from Him, but how we honor Him in how we treat one another. It has happened in my life as well. It is time to allow God to grant you peace and a walk in the Spirit that makes your enemies be at peace with you.

Reflection

Are there strained relationships in your life that God is calling you to entrust to Him?

How might the Lord be calling you to mark a boundary in peace rather than bitterness?

What does it look like to invite God to be the Witness between you and another?

Prayer: The Covenant of Peace

O God of Mizpah,
     You see what others cannot. You are the God who watches over the covenant,
     even when hearts part ways, even when trust has worn thin.
     Teach me to walk in the fear of the Lord,
     to forgive what I cannot fix,
     to bless what I no longer bear,
     and to release others to Your righteous care.
     Let the table I set today—whether in fellowship or in farewell—be seasoned with Your grace.
     Where I have held onto offense, loosen my grip.
     Where I have labored in bondage, give me freedom.
     And as I cross from one season into the next,
     mark the boundary with peace.
     You are the Witness between me and every person I leave in Your hands.
     Be glorified in my going and my returning.
     In Jesus' name, Amen.

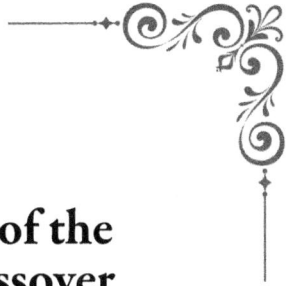

Day 3 – The Table of the Lord: The First Passover Meal

SCRIPTURE:

"¹¹And thus shall ye eat it; with your loins girded, your shoes on your feet, and your staff in your hand; and ye shall eat it in haste: it is the Lord's passover. ¹²For I will pass through the land of Egypt this night, ... and against all the gods of Egypt I will execute judgment: I am the Lord."

—Exodus 12:11–13 (KJV)

Devotional Meditation

On the night of deliverance, God did not raise an army—He prepared a table. The Passover meal, simple in its ingredients yet mighty in its meaning, was the turning point of a people bound in slavery. It wasn't just the lamb on the plate that mattered—it was the blood on the doorpost, the obedience of faith, and the gathering of families who dared to believe in God's promise of salvation.

This meal was eaten in haste, with shoes on and staff in hand, because God was about to move. The table of Passover was not about comfort—it was about covenant. It marked the beginning of Israel's freedom and their identity as a holy nation, purchased not with silver or gold, but with the blood of a spotless lamb.

The Lord's Table we now celebrate traces its roots to this sacred night. Jesus, our perfect Passover Lamb, was sacrificed during Passover week, fulfilling what the first table foreshadowed. As we remember this meal, we're not only looking back—we're entering into a holy continuity, from Egypt to Calvary to eternity.

The Passover table is the altar of our redemption. It reminds us that deliverance comes not by strength, but by surrender to the blood that speaks a better word than that of Abel. It is the blood that sets us free. You can rest in the liberty that the blood of the Covenant brings today. The blood of the Lamb makes remission for our sin. Surrender may be difficult but there is peace that passes understanding knowing your burdens belong to the Lamb.

Reflection

Are you still trying to win your freedom by your own effort, or are you resting in the Lamb who was slain?

What areas of your life need to come under the covering of the blood again today?

How can you keep your spiritual "sandals on"—ready for God's next move?

Prayer: Covered by the Blood

Father of Redemption,
You delivered Your people not with swords, but with a lamb.
You covered them not with shields, but with blood.
I thank You that my freedom does not depend on my ability,
but on Your mercy, poured out through Christ, my Passover Lamb.
Cover my heart afresh today with the blood that saves.
Let the doorposts of my life be marked with surrender.

Let every part of me be ready to move when You say go.
I choose obedience. I receive the Lamb.
I eat in faith, I walk in freedom,
and I trust You to bring me out of every bondage.
This table is holy because You are here.
Pass over me in mercy, and lead me into promise.
In Jesus' name, Amen.

Day 4 – A Table at Sinai: The Feast of Weeks and Glory

SCRIPTURE:

"⁹Then went up Moses, and Aaron, Nadab, and Abihu, and seventy of the elders of Israel: ¹⁰And they saw the God of Israel: .... also they saw God, and did eat and drink."
—Exodus 24:9–11 (KJV)

Devotional:

This is one of the most mysterious and sacred meals in all of Scripture. God has called Moses and the elders of Israel not just to witness His covenant—but to share a table in His presence. They became people governed by the Word.

He calls them up the mountain. He sets boundaries—because holiness is not casual, redemption is costly. Blood has just been sprinkled. The book has just been read. The sacrifice is still fresh on the altar. And then—He welcomes them.

"They saw the God of Israel."

What holy trembling must have filled the air! They didn't die. They weren't consumed. In the midst of fire, smoke, and thunder—God made a way for communion. That communion consummated a relationship. They were His.

And they ate.

And they drank.

This was more than nourishment—it was nearness. More than fellowship—it was friendship. God was not just making laws—He was making covenant. And in the sacred stillness of that mountain, He fed His leaders from His presence.

So it is with us. The blood of the Lamb has been poured. The Book has been read. And now, God calls us up—out of fear and into fellowship. He prepares a table not just to remember a transaction—but to renew a relationship. Set us apart in holiness. The signs of majesty followed. Voices, fire, and a trumpet. Yet in the midst of it all stood a meal. This is the covenant table—where presence meets promise.

And perhaps the greatest mystery of all:

They saw God...

And they ate and drank. Their communion became commitment. This communion was filled with the wonder of relationship. Consecration becomes commission. Redemption would be the outcome.

This was Divine love on display. God met them like he had never had before.

There the first Pentecost would happen and speak of another in the future. It was a new beginning. In your life today there are moments of divine nearness. Don't be afraid of commitment, consecration – it means revival is coming. He has placed his love upon you. Souls are waiting on you to approach the table in reverence and awe. Heaven is waiting on you. There is a cloud of witnesses cheering you forward. Revival is a relationship and it starts at the table.

Reflection:

Do I come to God's table casually, or do I come aware that it was prepared by blood?

What does it mean to see God and eat—to fellowship with Him not only in prayer but in presence?

Consecration and Commission - how do I see myself at His table?

Prayer:

L ord, I am in awe. That You would invite fragile dust like me to sit in Your presence and dine—what grace. You are holy, and yet You call me near. Thank You for the blood that opens the way. Thank You for Your covenant of love. Let every time I come to Your table be sacred. Let me see You again. And feed me—not just with bread, but with You. Amen

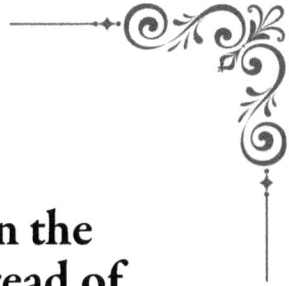

Day 5 – A Table in the Holy Place: The Bread of the Presence

SCRIPTURE:

"**30**And thou shalt set upon the table shewbread before me alway."
—Exodus 25:30

Devotional Meditation

In the holy place of the Tabernacle, just outside the veil of the Most Holy Place, stood a golden table. Upon it sat twelve loaves of bread, known as the Bread of the Presence—or in Hebrew, Lechem Panim, literally "the bread of the face." This was no ordinary bread. It represented the twelve tribes of Israel, continually before the face of God, sustained in His presence, covered by His covenant.

Every Sabbath, the bread was freshly replaced by the priests and eaten in the sacred space. It was a weekly reminder that life is sustained not by bread alone, but by being in communion with God. The bread didn't just symbolize provision—it signified proximity. Israel was a people meant to dwell in God's presence, not just survive in the wilderness.

In Christ, the Bread of Life, we are continually brought near. We no longer live at a distance—we've been invited to draw close. As we partake of Him, we are nourished not only in body, but in spirit. We become, like that bread, a people always before His face —seen, known, welcomed.

This table reminds us that revival isn't a one-time event. It is a life sustained in His presence, renewed each Sabbath, and consumed in worship.

Reflection

What would it look like for you to live "before His face" today?

Do you sense God calling you into deeper nearness—not just belief, but communion?

In what ways are you feeding your soul on the Bread of Life?

Prayer: The Face of God

Holy Father,
          You prepared a table in the sanctuary, not just for offerings, but for fellowship.

You longed for a people who would live before Your face.

And in Christ, You made a way for me to dwell in that holy place.

Thank You for the Bread of Presence that never grows stale, for the nearness that never fades,

and for the weekly reminder that I am Yours, and You are mine.

Draw me closer today. Let me feast not just on knowledge, but on You.

Renew my heart in Your presence.

Make my life a loaf set before You, holy, fragrant, and pleasing.

Let Your face shine upon me, and let me never hunger again.
In Jesus' name, Amen.

Day 6 – A Table of Peace:
The Fellowship Offering

SCRIPTURE:

"**3** And if his oblation be a sacrifice of peace offering, if he offer it of the herd ... And he shall lay his hand upon the head of his offering ³ And he shall offer of the sacrifice of the peace offering an offering made by fire unto the Lord; ⁹And he shall offer of the sacrifice of the peace offering an offering made by fire unto the Lord; ⁷It shall be a perpetual statute for your generations throughout all your dwellings," —Leviticus 3:1 -7 (selected)

Devotional Meditation

In the heart of Leviticus lies one of the most tender offerings in all of Scripture—the fellowship offering (zebach shelamim). It was not brought to atone for sin, but to celebrate peace, thanksgiving, or a vow fulfilled. It was a meal shared between God, the priest, and the worshiper—a sacred communion meal at the altar of the Lord.

Unlike the burnt offering, which was wholly consumed by fire, the fellowship offering was partly consumed by the priest, partly by the one who brought it, and part was given to God on the altar. It was a table of shared participation. A holy barbecue of covenant love.

The word shelamim is rooted in shalom—wholeness, peace, restoration. This offering symbolized restored relationship, harmony with God and man, and joyful communion. It was an altar of gratitude. A meal of unity.

Jesus, our peace offering, has made us whole. He has invited us to a table where sin is not just forgiven but where fellowship is restored. We are not merely tolerated—we are welcomed to feast in the presence of God. The fire of the altar still burns, but now it burns with acceptance, not wrath. The aroma of fellowship rises when hearts return to the Lord and share in His joy.

Reflection

Do you view your relationship with God as a burden or as fellowship?

In what ways are you expressing gratitude and restored peace through worship?

Is your life producing the aroma of peace—shalom—in your relationships and before the Lord?

Prayer: The Aroma of Fellowship

Lord Almighty,
You are not only a God who forgives—You are a God who feasts. You have made peace through the blood of the Lamb. Now You call me not just to serve, but to dine, to draw near, to delight in Your presence.

Burn away in me anything that disrupts our fellowship.
Let my worship rise like a pleasing aroma.
Make my life a table of peace and reconciliation.

Thank You for the fellowship offering—fulfilled in Christ, and poured into my soul.

I receive the gift of Your wholeness.

I bring You my gratitude.

And I welcome Your fire to fall again on the altar of my heart.

In Jesus' name, Amen.

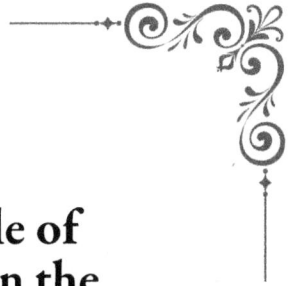

Day 7 – The Table of Aaron: The Fire on the Altar

SCRIPTURE:

"¹³The fire shall ever be burning upon the altar; it shall never go out" —Leviticus 6:13 (KJV)

Devotional Meditation

Before revival breaks out, the altar must burn.

In the tabernacle of Moses, the fire on the altar was not optional—it was perpetual. God Himself ignited the flame (Leviticus 9:24), but the priests were charged to keep it burning. This fire represented the presence of God, the consuming power of His holiness, and the ongoing sacrifice of a surrendered heart.

The altar was more than a place of death—it was the place of divine encounter. The offering was consumed, but glory descended. And from that holy fire, the people knew: God is with us.

Today, the altar is no longer made of bronze. It is your heart. It is your life. And the Lord still seeks those who will climb upon the altar, not with dead animals, but with living obedience (Romans 12:1). When we present ourselves fully to Him, His fire falls. And that fire doesn't destroy—it refines.

The fire on the altar is the flame of revival. It consumes sin, ignites worship, and empowers witness. Keep it burning. Feed it with prayer. Guard it with repentance. Fan it with praise.

Reflection

Is the fire of God still burning on the altar of your heart?

What are some practical ways you can keep the flame alive daily?

How is God calling you to offer yourself as a living sacrifice today?

Prayer: Let the Fire Fall

Holy God,
> You are a consuming fire.
You call me not to a cold religion,
but to a burning altar of love.
Ignite my heart again.
Let Your holy fire fall upon my life.
Consume what is not of You.
Purify what remains.
And kindle in me a passion for Your presence.
May I never let the fire go out.
May I tend the altar with reverence,
until the world sees Your glory in me.
In Jesus' name, Amen.

Day 8 - The Table and Humility: A Daily Renewal

SCRIPTURE:

"³And he humbled thee, and suffered thee to hunger, and fed thee with manna...that man doth not live by bread only, but by every word that proceedeth out of the mouth of the Lord ..."Deuteronomy 8:3

Devotional Meditation

The wilderness is not a place of lack—it's a place of training. A place of discipleship. A place of discipline. A place of relationship.

When Israel wandered in the desert, it was not because God abandoned them. It was because He was preparing them. Every morning, manna appeared—just enough for that day. It couldn't be stored, hoarded, or preserved. It had to be gathered fresh, in faith, each sunrise.

This was the table God spread in the wilderness: a daily bread, miraculous and mysterious, designed to teach dependence. It was not just to fill their stomachs but to awaken their souls. To train their hearts that the Table should never be neglected. Relationships must be kindled and kept. And so it is for us.

We often long for abundance, but God sometimes allows us to walk through seasons where we must rely on His Word like daily manna. He humbles us, not to hurt us, but to heal us from self-sufficiency. At the wilderness table, we learn again that every breath, every step, every crumb of grace comes from His faithful hand. This is holiness. This is walking in the Spirit.

The table in the wilderness is not glamorous—but it is sacred. It reminds us that we are not sustained by what we see, but by the unseen provision of our God.

Remind me O Lord that humility is the beauty of holiness. Following the Shepherd is the journey to joy. I am ready at Your Table.

Reflection

Are you in a wilderness season where God is teaching you to trust Him daily?

What daily manna—Word, encouragement, presence—has He been providing for you lately?

How might your dependence grow when you feast on His Word each morning?

Prayer: Daily Bread for My Soul

Faithful God,
    You fed Your people in the desert.
You sustained them with manna,
    and You are still feeding Your children today.
Help me to trust Your provision—day by day.
Help me not to worry about tomorrow,
    but to receive what You give with gratitude and faith.
When I feel dry, You are my source.

When I feel weak, You are my strength.
Speak, Lord—Your Word is my food.
Fill me again, morning by morning.
In Jesus' name, Amen.

Day 9 - The Table of the Promised Land: Grapes from Eschol

SCRIPTURE:

"²³And they came unto the brook of Eshcol, and cut down from thence a branch with one cluster of grapes, and they bare it between two upon a staff; and they brought of the pomegranates, and of the figs." —Numbers 13:23

Devotional Meditation

Twelve men entered the land.

Only two returned with grapes in their hands and faith in their hearts.

While the other ten spies saw giants, Joshua and Caleb saw a table set by God. They did not come back with fear or defeat. They didn't even bring back weapons or war plans. They brought back fruit.

And not just any fruit—a cluster of grapes so large it took two men to carry it.

This was more than produce. It was evidence of God's faithfulness. The land was not just filled with promise—it was rich with provision. The grapes of Eschol were a taste of the future—a sample of what God was about to pour out in full.

This is the table of the Promised Land: a place of prophetic tasting, a place of revival hunger, and a place where faith sees what fear cannot.

The Holy Spirit is our Eschol today. When we receive the Spirit's outpouring, we are tasting of the world to come. His joy is our strength. His gifts are our weapons. His presence is our nourishment.

Like Caleb and Joshua, we are not called to bring back tales of tragedy from this life—we are called to carry the fruit of the land. The Promise has power. We are called to be witnesses of what is possible when God goes before us.

So lift your eyes. Pick up your grapes. And bring back the taste of revival to a world bound in fear.

Reflection

What fruit has God already placed in your hands as a sign of His promises?

Are you living with a Caleb-spirit—faithful, hopeful, and bold in the face of giants?

How does the Holy Spirit serve as a foretaste of your eternal inheritance?

Prayer: Let Me Carry the Fruit of the Land

Faithful God,
 You've promised me a land of victory,
a place flowing with milk and honey.
But more than land, You've given me Your Spirit.
Let me taste what's coming.
Let me carry fruit from the future.
Let me walk like Caleb—with courage, with trust, and with joy.
Even when others doubt, I will believe.
Even when others retreat, I will press forward.
Make me a carrier of grapes—evidence that revival is real,

and that Your Spirit is more than enough.
In Jesus' name, Amen.

Day 10 - The Table of Gideon: Brokenness and Glory

SCRIPTURE:

"²²And the three hundred blew the trumpets, and the Lord set every man's sword against his fellow, even throughout all the host." —Judges 7:22

Devotional Meditation

Gideon was threshing wheat in hiding when the Angel of the Lord found him. He didn't feel like a warrior—he felt weak, unworthy, and unsure. Yet God called him mighty. And more than that—God invited him to a table of trust and obedience.

Before the battle, Gideon prepared an offering. The Angel touched it with His staff, and fire consumed it (Judges 6:21). That fire became the assurance of God's presence. From there, Gideon's journey would be marked not by strength but by surrender.

At the final battle, God reduced Gideon's army to just 300 men. No swords, no grand weapons. Just trumpets, clay jars, and torches. And then the jars were broken. Out of that brokenness came victory, as God confused the enemy and won the battle Himself.

The Table of Gideon and the Midianites is the table of brokenness that releases God's glory. It reminds us that our strength is not in numbers or skill—but in obedience and humility.

Sometimes revival starts not when we are strong, but when we are reduced—emptied of our own might, broken and available, holding only the torch of God's fire. It is in those moments that the enemy flees, and the name of the Lord is lifted high.

Reflection

What parts of your life feel broken or insufficient?
How might God be calling you to trust Him in weakness, not strength?
What does it mean to you that the battle belongs to the Lord?

Prayer: Break Me to Use Me

Lord of Hosts,
    You call the weak to victory,
the uncertain to trust,
the broken to glory.
I come with my clay jar,
fragile and flawed,
but I offer it to You.
Break me where I need breaking.
Let the light of Your presence shine out.
Win the battles I cannot win.
And let Your name be praised in my surrender.
I will follow, even with a torch and a trumpet.
You are enough.
In Jesus' name, Amen.

Day 11 - The Table of Manoah – Fire on the Offering

SCRIPTURE:

"**20**For it came to pass, when the flame went up toward heaven from off the altar, that the angel of the Lord ascended in the flame of the altar. And Manoah and his wife looked on it, and fell on their faces to the ground." —Judges 13:20

Devotional Meditation

B efore there was Samson, there was a barren woman and a praying husband. There was a visitation from heaven. And there was an offering laid on the rock.

Manoah and his wife didn't fully understand who stood before them—it was the Angel of the Lord. But their response was to worship, to bring a sacrifice, and to seek understanding. When the fire touched the offering, something holy happened: the angel ascended in the flame, and heaven kissed earth. They stood in the blaze of a covenant promise. A moment of sacred silence. A moment of Wonder.

This was not just a miracle—it was an invitation.

The Table of Manoah is a place of divine encounter where the offering is accepted, and the messenger is revealed. God's Name is known. It is where fear turns into faith, where barrenness becomes hope, and where the Lord affirms His call.

Some of the deepest revivals in Scripture began with one household, one altar, one encounter, and a meal.

God still meets His people around altars of consecration. When we offer ourselves in surrender, and when we honor His presence, He responds with fire. Not always visible, but unmistakably real. His Name will be given to us there. It is Wonderful, Counsellor, Mighty God, the Everlasting Father, and the Prince of Peace.

This table calls us to seek Him not only for what He will do in the future—but for who He is right now. We are called to revival. Give yourself in consecration. The fire always falls.

Reflection

What would it look like to prepare a sacred table of worship in your home?

In what areas of your life is God asking you to lay down a fresh offering?

How does this story invite you into deeper expectancy for God's presence?

Prayer: Let the Fire Fall Again

Lord of Glory,
   You visit the humble,
You respond to worship,
You ignite the altar with Your fire.
Let my life be like Manoah's rock—
a place where Your presence is welcomed,
where my offering is laid in love,
and where heaven is revealed.
I long not just for answers,
but for You.
Let my worship be pure,

my surrender be real,
and my heart be open to holy encounter.
Fall again, Lord.
Let the flame rise.
Let revival begin.
In Jesus' name, Amen.

Day 12- The Table of Strength: Honey from the Lion

SCRIPTURE:

"**14**And he said unto them, Out of the eater came forth meat, and out of the strong came forth sweetness. And they could not in three days expound the riddle." —Judges 14:14

Devotional Meditation

Samson returned to the place of his former battle and found something unexpected.

Honey.

Not in a jar. Not in a hive.

But inside the carcass of the lion he had once killed.

Out of what had once been a place of death, God had caused sweetness to flow. What was meant to devour Samson became a table of strength. It was more than a riddle—it was a revelation. It was revival.

This is the table of strength.

Sometimes God lets us revisit the places of our greatest warfare—not to grieve, but to receive nourishment. The scars on your life are not just reminders of what hurt you—they are testimonies of what didn't destroy you. They are mountains to climb on.

There is honey hidden in the victory.

The lion is dead, but the sweetness of God is alive. Paul said, "He always causes us to triumph through Jesus Christ the Lord".

When we walk in obedience—even if flawed obedience like Samson's—God has a way of redeeming. God has a way of making the bitter things sweet. He has a plan. What was once a battlefield becomes a banquet hall for the soul.

Reflection

• What former battles has God used to strengthen and sweeten your walk with Him?

• Can you recognize any "honey in the carcass" experiences in your life?

• What does this teach you about how God brings redemption from struggle?

Prayer: Let Me Taste the Strength You've Given Me

Mighty God,
You turn battlefields into places of sweetness.
You turn what tried to kill me into what now nourishes me.
Thank You for the honey in hard places.
Thank You for the strength that flows from former wounds.
Let me walk forward in Your strength.
Help me see Your provision, even when it comes in unexpected forms.
Make me one who feeds on Your victory
and lives with revived faith.
In Jesus' name, Amen.

Day 13 - The Table of the Jawbone: Thirst and Deliverance

SCRIPTURE:

"¹⁸And he was sore athirst, and called on the Lord, and said, Thou hast given this great deliverance into the hand of thy servant: and now shall I die for thirst... ¹⁹But God clave an hollow place that was in the jaw, and there came water thereout; and when he had drunk, his spirit came again, and he revived...." —Judges 15:18–19

Devotional Meditation

Samson had just won a miraculous victory. With only a donkey's jawbone, he had slain a thousand men. But achieving victory means we have spent our strength.

In the quiet aftermath of battle, thirst hit him hard—a thirst so deep it brought him to the edge of death. And it was there, in weakness, that Samson did something rarely recorded of him: he prayed.

He cried out to the Lord.

And the Lord answered.

God opened a hollow place in the jawbone, and from it flowed reviving water. In that moment, Samson drank not only water, but grace. He discovered the God who gives victory is also the God who sustains through mercy. This grace is required for continued victory.

The Table of Samson and the Jawbone is a Table of Divine Provision in your weakness. It teaches us that even after great triumphs, we are still dependent. Even when we've walked in strength, we still need the refreshing stream of the Spirit. God is here. He will refresh you. He will fill you. He will answer you.

How does He do that? Through the Spirit and the Word. That is what we see here in the Mystery of the Jawbone. The new consecration of the Spirit and the Word – the jawbone came from the sacrifice of a donkey from Exodus 34:20. It wasn't an old jawbone but a new one – a new consecration. This consecration brought life to a man who needed spiritual renewal and refreshment.

We may not face enemies with weapons, we all face spiritual battles daily—and the victories can leave us thirsty, drained, and weary. This table is for all who've fought hard and now need to drink deep. God says - "Everyone who is thirsty, let him drink!"

Come to the Lord. He will fill the hollow place of your heart, the Word will heal and rivers will flow. He has a Table after the victory.

Reflection

- Have you ever felt weary after a spiritual battle—even after a victory?
- What does Samson's prayer teach you about dependence on God?
- Where is the Lord inviting you to drink again and be revived?

Prayer: Refresh My Soul Again

God of My Strength,
You are the One who gives victory,
and the One who gives water.
Without You, I am dry.

Without You, I cannot endure.
Open the hollow place in me.
Let Your Spirit pour out fresh life.
Quench my thirst, renew my strength,
revive my heart.
Even in my victories, remind me I need You.
Keep me dependent.
Keep me surrendered.
And keep me close to the Rock that refreshes.
In Jesus' name, Amen.

Part 2 - Continued

Scripture:

"^{28}And Samson called unto the Lord, and said, O Lord God, remember me, I pray thee, and strengthen me, I pray thee, only this once, O God, that I may be at once avenged of the Philistines for my two eyes.'" —Judges 16:28

Devotional Meditation

Few stories in Scripture strike the heart like Samson's.

Called from birth. Set apart by a Nazarite vow. Empowered by the Spirit. And yet—he fell. He gave away the secret of his strength. He was blinded, bound, and broken. And for a moment, it seemed like the end.

But grace writes a different ending. It always does for the repentant heart.

In the final scene of Samson's life, we see a man no longer relying on his might but leaning entirely on the mercy of God. There, at the table of his weakness, strength returned. Not from within, but from above. Not through raw display of power, but of raw honesty and dependence.

This was Samson's table with the Lord—not a feast of food, but a feast of grace. A moment of repentance. A prayer of surrender. One final act of obedience that brought victory.

This table reminds us: It's never too late to return. God's mercy reaches the lowest places. His strength is made perfect in our weakness. And even after failure, He prepares a table where redemption flows. It was Samson's greatest victory yet. It is not over. From God's standpoint your victory is just begun!

Reflection

- Have you ever felt like your mistakes disqualified you from God's purpose?

- What does Samson's story teach you about the mercy and strength of God?

- How can you return to the table today—even if you've fallen?

Prayer: Strengthen Me Once More

Merciful Father,
      You see me when I am strong,
and You hold me when I am weak.
Like Samson, I've missed it.
I've failed. I've wandered.
But Your grace invites me still.
Remember me, Lord.
Strengthen me once more.
Let my final chapter be full of purpose,
not shame.
Let my surrender become my victory.
I trust in Your mercy.
I feast at Your table—
a table of restoration and redeeming love.
In Jesus' name, Amen.

Day 14 - The Table of Jonathan: A Warrior's Honey in the Heights

SCRIPTURE:

"²⁷But Jonathan....put forth the end of the rod that was in his hand, and dipped it in an honeycomb, and put his hand to his mouth; and his eyes were enlightened"—1 Samuel 14:27

Devotional Meditation

The army was exhausted. Bound by a rash oath from Saul, no one dared to eat. But Jonathan—unaware of the command—found honey on the battlefield, and when he tasted it, his eyes brightened.

In the midst of warfare, God had provided sweetness. The honey was not just a gift of strength—it was a sign of God's presence in the heights.

The Table of Jonathan is a table for those who dare to climb in faith. He and his armor-bearer had said, "Perhaps the Lord will act on our behalf." With nothing but faith, they ascended the cliffs and defeated the enemy. But after the battle, came the honey—the reminder that God not only gives victory, but refreshes the weary soul.

When others are fainting from religious pressure or human mandates, those who walk in the Spirit find strength in what God provides. Honey in the heights—supernatural strength in the high places of battle.

Jonathan's heart was already bold. He had just declared, "Nothing can hinder the Lord from saving, whether by many or by few." He believed. And when he tasted the honey, his courage was renewed and confirmed.

There is a kind of strength that only comes from doing what is right when no one else will. Jonathan's act wasn't rebellion—it was revival. A taste of what God had placed along the path.

For us, this honey is the Word of God. It is the Spirit's whisper in the shadows. It is joy in the midst of fatigue. And it is courage to keep climbing, even when the world says, "Sit down."

You may be in the middle of a steep climb, facing pressure, fatigue, and spiritual warfare. But don't miss the honey God has placed along the way. His Word is sweet. His presence is reviving. And one taste from Him can brighten your eyes again.

Reflection

Where in your life are you feeling battle-weary or spiritually tired?

What "honey" has God placed along your path that you may have overlooked?

How can you make room for divine refreshment in the middle of your climb?

Prayer: Sweeten My Strength Again

Father of the Heights,
You go before me into every battle.
You call me to climb in faith,
and You meet me on the mountain.
Thank You for the honey of Your Word.
Thank You for the sweetness of Your presence.
Even in war, You provide refreshment.

Brighten my eyes again.
Strengthen my heart.
Revive my steps.
And let me never fight in my own strength,
but in the joy that comes from You.
In Jesus' name, Amen.

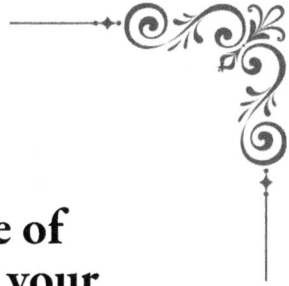

Day 15 - A Table of Abigail: God sees your sacrifice.

SCRIPTURE:

"**8**Then Abigail made haste, and took two hundred loaves, and two bottles of wine, and five sheep ready dressed, and five measures of parched corn, and an hundred clusters of raisins, and two hundred cakes of figs, and laid them on asses. and, behold, David and his men came down against her; and she met them. because my lord fighteth the battles of the Lord, and evil hath not been found in thee all thy days. **30**And it shall come to pass, when the Lord shall have done to my lord according to all the good that he hath spoken concerning thee, and shall have appointed thee ruler over Israel; Please forgive the trespass of your servant. For the LORD will certainly make my lord a sure house, because my lord is fighting the battles of the LORD, and evil shall not be found in you as long as you live" —1 Samuel 25 (selected)

Devotional Meditation

David had been faithful. He had been true. Now he is betrayed.
He had served in the shadows. He had protected Nabal's flocks in the wilderness, offering care and vigilance without asking for payment—only honor.

57

But instead of gratitude, he was met with scorn. Betrayed by a fool, his heart burned with righteous anger. He wasn't just hurt—he was ready to retaliate.

And yet, the Lord intervened.

God, in His mercy, met David not with rebuke—but with a table. He prepared a feast for His weary servant in the very place of betrayal. A meal was laid out in the wilderness—not by accident, but by divine design. The bread and wine that came to David were not just provision—they were a reminder. He had to do the unthinkable. Forgive their folly. Restrain your vengeance. Allow God to reign.

A reminder that God sees your pain.

A reminder that the Lord is your Defender.

A reminder that He sets a table in your betrayal, not to vindicate you in vengeance, but to restore you in calling.

This is the table of quiet revival in the middle of battle. This is the table that says, "I still see you. I still anoint you. I still have more for you." Right in the middle of the betrayal of Nabal - God confirms His calling of David and renews courage. Take courage my friend. God will strengthen you again.

Reflection

Have you recently walked through a season of betrayal or dishonor?

In what ways has God quietly provided for you when you could have responded in anger or bitterness?

What does it mean for God to prepare a table in the presence of your enemies?

Prayer: You Set My Table in Betrayal

Faithful Shepherd,
   You know the sting of betrayal.
You see what others never saw.
And still, You prepare a table for me.
Not a table of revenge—but a table of peace.
You restore my dignity,
You remind me of my calling,
You anoint my head with oil.
Feed me when I feel forgotten.
Strengthen me where I'm tempted to quit.
Let my cup overflow again with trust, with mercy, and with purpose.
Thank You for setting a table in my betrayal—
A place of rest. A place of healing. A place of revival.
In Jesus' name, Amen.

Day 16 - The King's Table: Covenant Kindness

SCRIPTURE:

"⁷And David said unto him, Fear not: for I will surely shew thee kindness for Jonathan thy father's sake, and will restore thee all the land of Saul thy father; and thou shalt eat bread at my table continually.."
—2 Samuel 9:7

Devotional Meditation

Mephibosheth was forgotten. Lame in both feet, he lived in Lo-Debar—a place of no pasture, no promise, no peace. The grandson of a fallen king, he had every reason to fear when summoned by David, Israel's reigning monarch. Yet instead of punishment, he received restoration. Instead of rejection, he was given a seat at the King's table.

This moment wasn't about Mephibosheth's worthiness—it was about covenant. David had made a vow to Jonathan, and covenant love never forgets. Kindness *(chesed)* found Mephibosheth in his weakness and carried him to a place of honor.

The King's table is a place of dignity for the broken. It is where fear is silenced by grace. Where shame is covered by restoration. Where orphans eat like sons. David didn't just feed Mephibosheth—he gave him a permanent seat, a lifelong welcome.

This is our story. Christ, the Greater David, has called us out of spiritual barrenness and seated us with Him in heavenly places. We are no longer castoffs—we are covenant children. And the table He sets is not temporary. His banner over us is love, and His kindness has no end. Our King says, "You will sit with me always."

Reflection

- Have you ever felt like Mephibosheth—forgotten, unworthy, or broken?
- What does the kindness of God mean to you personally today?
- How can you extend the same covenant kindness to others in your life?

Prayer: A Seat at the Table

King Jesus,
    You found me when I had nothing.
You called me when I was hiding.
And You welcomed me when I had no strength to walk.
Thank You for the covenant that carried me to grace.
Thank You for the kindness that restores my name,
and for the seat You have prepared at Your table.
Let me never take Your mercy for granted.
Let me live as a child of the King.
And let my life extend this kindness to others,
so they too may know the welcome of heaven's banquet.
In Your Name, Amen.

Day 17 – The Table of Mephibosheth: The Approval of the King

SCRIPTURE:

"**11**... According to all that my lord the king hath commanded his servant, so shall thy servant do. As for Mephibosheth, said the king, he shall eat at my table, as one of the king's sons." —2 Samuel 9:11

Devotional Meditation

Mephibosheth had no claim to favor. Crippled by a fall at birth, living in obscurity, the grandson of Saul had nothing to offer the king. Yet David sought him out—not to condemn, but to restore, and remember. He brought Mephibosheth to his palace and gave him a seat at the king's table—not for a visit, but for life.

This is a picture of the gospel.

We, too, were crippled—broken by the fall, living far from God, without hope or inheritance. But the Son of David came looking for us. Not because of our worthiness, but because of His covenant love. Like David's kindness to Jonathan, God remembers His promises and pours out mercy on the undeserving. We are no longer strangers but sons.

The King's Table is not reserved for the flawless—it's prepared for the redeemed. When we sit with Jesus, we are no longer defined by our past, our pain, or our paralysis. We are seated as sons and daughters of the King.

Even with our limp, He makes us part of the royal family. Here is the best part- at His Table everyone is equal. Seated there your limp can't be seen. Your weakness is covered by His Strength. Rest at the Table today.

Reflection

Have you ever felt like Mephibosheth—ashamed, unworthy, or forgotten?

What does it mean to you that God invites you to sit at His table like one of His own children?

How can you reflect that same covenant kindness to someone else today?

Prayer: Seat Me at Your Table

King of Kings,
I come like Mephibosheth—limping, undeserving, and amazed by Your kindness.
You have sought me out when I was hiding.
You have lifted me from shame and seated me in honor.
Thank You for the table You've prepared.
Thank You for making me family, not a guest.
I receive Your mercy with wonder.
Help me extend that same grace to others.
Let my life be a testimony of covenant love—
a story of what only the King could do.
In Jesus' name, Amen.

Day 18– The Prophet's Table: Elijah and the Meal of Strength

SCRIPTURE:

"**5**And as he lay and slept under a juniper tree, behold, then an angel touched him, and said unto him, Arise and eat. **6**And he looked, and, behold, there was a cake baken on the coals, and a cruse of water at his head. And he did eat and drink, and laid him down again." —1 Kings 19:5–6

Devotional Meditation

Elijah had just called down fire from heaven—and now, he lay under a broom tree, weary, afraid, and ready to die. The prophet who once stood boldly now whispers despair. But God, in mercy, does not rebuke him. He bakes him bread.

This is the kindness of the Lord—the God who knows when our souls are spent. He sends an angel not with a sword, but with a meal. Not with correction, but with compassion. "Arise and eat," the angel says, "for the journey is too great for you."

And Elijah is sustained—not by a feast, but by the bread of heaven.

The Table of the Lord is not only for celebration—it is for our restoration. It is where God meets you in your wilderness. He feeds you when you're too tired to go on. He strengthens you for the next step, even if all you can do now is rest. Refreshment came after the victory. God wants you to hear His voice. He is not finished with you yet. This is not the end. It is the beginning.

When you feel empty, afraid, exhausted - He is there. Do you feel discouragement, the Lord prepares a table. He knows what you need. And He will carry you through the journey ahead. He has a message for you. Come to the Table. It is time to dine.

Reflection

Can you recall a time when God ministered to you in a season of exhaustion or discouragement?

What might it look like to receive God's rest and strength today, even in your weakness?

How can you offer bread and kindness to someone who may be walking through their own valley?

Prayer: Feed Me Again, Lord

God of Comfort,
    You know my frame.
You see my weariness.
And You come—not to crush me, but to care for me.
Thank You for bread in the wilderness.
Thank You for rest when I have no strength left.
Help me to receive what You offer,
to rise when You call,
and to walk again—nourished by Your grace.

Feed me again, Lord.
Until I reach the mountain of Your presence.
Amen.

Day 19 - A Table of Rest: Elijah's Meal of Renewal

SCRIPTURE:

"⁷And the angel of the Lord came again the second time, and touched him, and said, Arise and eat; because the journey is too great for thee. ⁸And he arose, and did eat and drink, and went in the strength of that meat forty days and forty nights unto Horeb the mount of God.." —1 Kings 19:5–6

Devotional Meditation

Elijah was done. The fire had fallen on Mount Carmel, the prophets of Baal were defeated, but Queen Jezebel's threats pierced him deeper than the sword. Fleeing into the wilderness, Elijah collapsed under a broom tree and begged God to take his life. This was not just exhaustion—it was despair. The mighty prophet was empty.

And how did God respond? Not with rebuke, not with commands—but with a meal. Bread baked on hot stones. Water in a jar. The Angel of the Lord touched him and said, "Get up and eat." Not once, but twice.

The table in the wilderness is not just a table of victory—it's the table of restoration. When your soul is weary, when the journey feels too much, God meets you not with questions, but with nourishment. He feeds the broken. He prepares a table not just in the presence of enemies—but in the presence of despair.

This meal didn't end the battle, but it gave Elijah strength to carry on. He walked forty days and nights on the strength of that food—into a cave, into a whisper, into a fresh commission.

Even prophets need to be fed. Even revivalists need rest. And even in the wilderness, God is still setting the table. The wind is hushed and the storm is gone but the Table kept him marching onward. Receive the bread from heaven today. Let him heal you!

Reflection

- Where in your life do you feel weary, empty, or burned out?
- What does it mean to receive God's rest and nourishment without guilt?
- Will you allow the Lord to feed your soul before you continue the journey?

Prayer: Bread in the Wilderness

Faithful God,
    You meet me not only on mountains, but in the valleys.
Not only in fire, but in stillness.
And when I feel too tired to go on, You prepare a table.
Thank You for the bread of restoration.
Thank You for feeding me when I can't feed myself.
Strengthen me again—not to strive, but to follow.
Not to perform, but to walk in step with You.
Touch me again with Your mercy.
Bake the bread over heavenly coals.
Give me living water for the road ahead.
And when I rise, let it be in Your strength, for Your glory.
In Jesus' name, Amen.

Day 20 – The Table of Oil: Anointed for His Purpose

SCRIPTURE:

"⁵... thou anointest my head with oil; my cup runneth over."
—Psalm 23:5b

Devotional Meditation

At the Shepherd's table, something sacred happens—He doesn't just feed you; He anoints you.

Oil in Scripture is more than a symbol of refreshment or healing—it represents the anointing of the Holy Spirit, the setting apart of one for a divine purpose. Kings were anointed with oil. Priests were consecrated with it. Prophets were set apart by it. And in Christ, we too are anointed with the oil of heaven to walk in our calling.

David declares, "You anoint my head with oil," not at a palace, but at a table—in the middle of the valley. It is not the absence of trouble but the presence of purpose that marks this moment.

God anoints you not when the battle ends, but often while it still rages—because His Spirit is your strength. His presence is your portion. His power is your overflow.

You were made to live anointed—not only to be comforted but to be commissioned. The Shepherd fills your cup, not to satisfy only you, but to overflow into the lives of others.

Reflection

Do you recognize the anointing of God in your life even in difficult places?

How does knowing you are anointed change how you walk through daily life?

Who around you needs the overflow of your cup today?

Prayer: Anoint Me Again

Shepherd of My Soul,
    You feed me, and You anoint me.
Even in the valley, You declare Your purpose over my life.
Your Spirit is my strength.
Your oil is my calling.
Fill my cup again, Lord.
Let it overflow with love, wisdom, and power.
Let my life bring healing to others,
and my table become a place of divine refreshment.
I receive Your anointing anew.
Set me apart for Your will,
and walk with me every step of the way.
In Jesus' name, Amen.

Day 21 – The Shepherd's Table: Heaven's Hospitality

SCRIPTURE:

"⁵Thou preparest a table before me in the presence of mine enemies: thou anointest my head with oil; my cup runneth over."
—Psalm 23:5

Devotional Meditation

In the middle of conflict, chaos, and dark valleys, the Good Shepherd spreads a table. Not in retreat, not in fear—but in the presence of enemies. This is the radical hospitality of heaven: peace in the midst of battle, abundance in the face of lack, rest in the presence of threat. God is not moved by your enemies and neither should you be.

Psalm 23 is not a psalm of naïve comfort. It is a warrior's song of trust. David, who faced lions, giants, and betrayal, wrote these words with battle-worn faith. And still, he declares: "You prepare a table for me." God is not only our refuge—He is our Host. He doesn't just defend; He nourishes, restores, and fills.

This table is not one of escape, but of presence. It doesn't mean the enemies are gone—it means they no longer have power over your joy. Right in the midst of turmoil, God nourishes you. He anoints you. He fills your cup until it overflows. This is the Shepherd's defense against despair.

The Shepherd's Table is where fear is quieted, identity is affirmed, and strength is renewed. It reminds us that God doesn't just deliver us from trouble—He sits with us through it. He is not just the Shepherd of green pastures, but of dark valleys too. And at His table, even in hardship, you are honored, chosen, and overflowing.

The Shepherd doesn't remove us from every storm. Instead, He sets the table in the storm and calls us to sit. He anoints our heads with oil—healing, consecration, dignity. He fills our cups with more than enough—joy, peace, His own presence.

When we feast with the Shepherd, we live above the fear of scarcity. We learn to eat in faith, to drink in trust, and to rest—even when the wolves are near. The Shepherd's table is where enemies become powerless and His goodness becomes overwhelming.

Reflection

What 'enemies' are you facing right now—fear, lack, anxiety, spiritual attack?

Can you see the table God is preparing for you, even in this valley?

How is He anointing and filling you in this season?

Prayer: The Table in the Valley

Shepherd of My Soul,
    Even when I walk through the darkest valley,

You are with me. You fight for me.
And You prepare a table that silences every lie.
Let me sit at Your table today.
Feed me with Your Word. Fill my cup with Your Spirit.
Anoint me again with fresh oil—oil of joy, healing, and power.
I will not fear what surrounds me.
My eyes are on the Shepherd.
My soul will feast, my heart will overflow,
and Your goodness will follow me all the days of my life.
In Jesus' name, Amen.

Day 22: Naboth's Table: The Inheritance We Cannot Trade Away

SCRIPTURE:

"And Naboth said to Ahab, The LORD forbid it me, that I should give the inheritance of my fathers unto thee."

— 1 Kings 21:3 (KJV)

Devotional

The story of Naboth is tucked quietly into 1 Kings 21, yet it resounds with the thunder of covenant truth. King Ahab looked at Naboth's vineyard and saw nothing more than convenience: a patch of fertile land near his palace. But Naboth looked at the same vineyard and saw the nachalah (נַחֲלָה)—the inheritance of his fathers, his covenant portion from God.

In the Law of Moses, God had said: "The land shall not be sold for ever: for the land is mine" (Leviticus 25:23). Every family's plot was their sacred share in the covenant. To give it away was to despise what God had given. Naboth understood this. He wasn't merely guarding property; he was honoring Adonai's design. To yield his inheritance would be to betray not just his ancestors, but the covenant itself.

Ahab offered Naboth what looked like a generous deal: "I'll give you a better vineyard in exchange, or I'll buy it for silver." But Naboth's reply was simple and immovable: "The LORD forbid it me." In Hebrew- it carries the weight of an oath—"Far be it from me, by the LORD's own Name, to surrender what He has given."

This was not stubbornness. It was faith. It was reverence. It was covenant loyalty. Naboth's table was the table of God's inheritance, and he would not sell it for comfort, convenience, or coin.

But Jezebel—driven by lawlessness (avlah) and idolatry—plotted Naboth's death. She raised up false witnesses (edim sheker), manipulated the elders, and had him stoned. In the natural, Naboth lost his vineyard and his life. Yet in the Spirit, his faithfulness shook the heavens. For the word of the Lord came to Elijah: "Hast thou killed, and also taken possession? ... In the place where dogs licked the blood of Naboth shall dogs lick thy blood, even thine" (1 Kings 21:19). The inheritance of God cannot be stolen without consequence.

The Prophetic Table

Naboth's vineyard is more than an ancient field—it is a prophetic picture of our inheritance in Christ. Through the blood of Yeshua, we have received yerushah olam—an eternal inheritance (Ephesians 1:11; Hebrews 9:15). Our vineyard is salvation, the anointing of the Spirit, the gifts of God, the calling upon our lives, our families, our spiritual legacy.

The enemy, like Ahab, still comes to bargain. He whispers:

◇ "Trade your integrity for success."
◇ "Sell your calling for comfort."
◇ "Exchange your holiness for pleasure."

And when bargaining fails, Jezebel still schemes—false accusation, persecution, pressure to silence and conform. Yet the call of Naboth rings across the centuries: "The LORD forbid it me."

The vineyard of the Lord is not for sale. The inheritance of the saints cannot be compromised. The table of inheritance must be guarded.

Revival Insight

Revival always calls the Church back to its inheritance. Not to trade it for worldly approval, not to sell it for silver, but to cherish it as holy. In days of pressure and compromise, Naboth's table teaches us that what God has entrusted must be honored—even at great cost. And just as God vindicated Naboth with prophetic judgment on Ahab and Jezebel, so He will vindicate His people who guard their inheritance in Christ.

This is the call of the hour: to take our place at the table of inheritance and say with unwavering faith, "I will not trade away what belongs to my Father. This portion is mine, sealed in the blood of Jesus, and I will cherish it as holy."

Reflection Questions

1. What is your nachalah—your God-given inheritance—that the enemy most tempts you to compromise or surrender?

2. How does Naboth's refusal to sell his vineyard speak to the modern Church, which often feels pressure to trade holiness for influence, or truth for acceptance?

3. How can you actively guard your vineyard and steward it faithfully, knowing it belongs not just to you, but to the Lord?

Prayer

Father of Abraham, Isaac, and Jacob,

Thank You for the inheritance You have given me in Christ—my salvation, my calling, my vineyard of promise. Forgive me for the times I have treated it lightly. Strengthen me with faith to guard what is holy and to resist every bargain of the enemy. May I echo Naboth's words, "The LORD forbid it me," whenever compromise comes to my door. Let my life become a table of inheritance, where Your promises are honored, Your portion is protected, and Your glory is revealed. In Yeshua's name, Amen

Day 23 - A Table of Isaiah's Prophecy: Feast of Victory

SCRIPTURE:

"[6]And in this mountain shall the Lord of hosts make unto all people a feast of fat things, a feast of wines on the lees...[8]He will swallow up death in victory; and the Lord God will wipe away tears from off all faces...[9]And it shall be said in that day, Lo, this is our God; we have waited for him, and he will save us: this is the Lord; we have waited for him, we will be glad and rejoice in his salvation.." —Isaiah 25:6, 8, 9

Devotional Meditation

Isaiah lifts the veil of time and sees a banquet not yet served—but already promised. On a holy mountain, the Lord prepares a table—not for Israel alone, but for all peoples. A feast of rich food, aged wine, and eternal hope. This is no ordinary meal. This is the final celebration—the end of death, the drying of tears, the vindication of those who've waited on the Lord.

This table is set by God Himself. No human hands can prepare such a feast. It is the culmination of every covenant, every prophetic longing, every sacrifice offered in faith. It is the soul's reward of redemption. Resurrection! The ultimate victory. Separation is no more. No more tears. The battle is over.

Isaiah doesn't just see what's served—he sees what's swallowed. "He will swallow up death forever." This meal follows victory, not trial. The last enemy is defeated, and joy takes its eternal seat. Sorrow is silenced. Shame is forgotten. And around the table are the faces of those who trusted Him through the night. His covenant is sure.

Every table we set in faith today points to this one. Every communion meal, every act of repentance, every moment of worship—it's all a foretaste of the day when the Lamb becomes the Host, and the nations rejoice. The last enemy is defeated by redemption, the promise of total victory. Isaiah saw a resurrection realized. He saw a future bright with promises. Open your eyes. Your enemies are defeated. This is our destiny today in Jesus Name!

Reflection

• When you think about the ultimate victory of God, what emotions or longings stir within you?

• How does this vision of the final feast give you strength to endure today's battles?

• In what ways can you reflect the joy of that coming day in your current life?

Prayer: A Place at the Feast

Lord of Glory,
You are preparing a table beyond my imagination.

You have planned a feast where death will be no more.
And You have saved me a seat through the blood of the Lamb.
Help me live today in light of that day.
Let hope rise in my heart even in the face of sorrow.
Let joy overflow, knowing that the tears of this life
will one day be wiped away forever.
Teach me to taste heaven now—
to rejoice, to worship, to persevere.
And when I falter, remind me again:
The feast is coming. The Lamb has triumphed.
And I will eat with You in joy.
In Jesus' name, Amen.

Day 24 - A Table of Esther: The Place of Reversal

SCRIPTURE:

"And Esther answered, If it seem good unto the king, let the king and Haman come this day unto the banquet that I have prepared for him."

— Esther 5:4 (KJV)

Devotional Meditation

A banquet doesn't sound like a simple meal, does it? But this was no ordinary feast. It couldn't have been as lavish as the one that opened the book of Esther, when the king displayed his glory for 180 days. Esther's banquet was smaller, more intimate, and more purposeful. It was a table she prepared with prayer, fasting, and courage.

The Hebrew word for banquet, mishteh (מִשְׁתֶּה), means a drinking feast—a covenant moment more than just a meal. Esther understood that this was not about splendor but about strategy. It was about God's providence - His sovereign weaving of every detail.

Haman, blinded by pride, thought his invitation was an honor. He boasted to his family, "Yea, Esther the queen did let no man come in with the king unto the banquet that she had prepared but myself" (Esther 5:12). He thought he was being exalted, but in truth, the table was about to expose him.

Because the table always reveals the heart. It tells us who we are – and it tells us who our enemies are.

◇ Haman's heart: wicked, murderous, swollen with pride.
◇ The king's heart: moved by love for his bride.
◇ Esther's heart: full of trust and favor born from intimacy.

Before she ever prepared the table, Esther entered hidden intercession. She fasted (tzom), she prayed (tefillah), and she called her people into agreement (am echad—one people). And God, who sees in secret, rewarded her openly.

At that table of reversal, the decree of death was overturned. Haman's gallows became his grave. The king's presence turned the banquet into breakthrough.

Beloved, this is our hope too. Every time we come to the Shulchan Adonai (Table of the Lord), we don't come to ritual but to Presence. And the presence of the King makes all the difference. At His table, decrees of death are broken, enemies fall, and new life is sealed for His people.

The table of Esther reminds us: where the King is present, the table becomes the place of reversal.

Reflection

1. Where in your life have you felt the "Haman plots" of the enemy rising against you? How does the story of Esther's table encourage you to trust in God's reversal?

2. Esther prepared her banquet with prayer, fasting, and intimacy with the king. How can you "prepare the table" of your heart in similar ways this week?

3. The presence of the King made all the difference at Esther's table. How can you deepen your intimacy with King Jesus so that your expectation of His intervention grows?

P **rayer:**
     King Jesus,

Thank You for inviting me to Your table. Let it be for me the table of reversal—the place where hidden intercession meets open reward, where pride is humbled, and where Your love seals life for Your people. I rest in Your lovingkindness, I trust in Your presence, and I believe that every decree of death is overturned by Your word of life. You have reversed and exposed my enemies. I come against pride, jealously, and all the selfishness of the enemy. I claim your Word – Your promises – Your life. My heart and love are yours. You protect me and You direct me. Amen.

Day 25 - The Table of Warning: The Return

SCRIPTURE:

"⁷Ye offer polluted bread upon mine altar... In that ye say, The table of the Lord is contemptible....¹⁰Who is there even among you that would shut the doors for nought? neither do ye kindle fire on mine altar for nought.'" —Malachi 1:7,10

Devotional Meditation

There is a soberness that must accompany any conversation about the table of the Lord.

Throughout this journey, we have tasted of grace, we've feasted on promises, and we've been invited deeper into communion and covenant. But Malachi's words pierce through the warmth with prophetic fire.

The priesthood in his day had become careless—offering blind animals, blemished sacrifices, and cold worship. And God, in His mercy, called them out. He cried, 'Shut the doors!'—not because He rejected worship, but because He longed for it to be pure. This was not the anger of a distant God. This was the passionate grief of a Father who knew what He deserved and what His people had forgotten.

The Table of Warning becomes a table of mercy. It is a Table of Dedication. It reminds us that God does not abandon us to our lukewarmness—He confronts it with glory. He beckons us to rise, to return, and to offer what is worthy of His name.

This is revival. Not emotionalism or performance, but the heart returning to the altar with tears and awe, giving God not our leftovers, but our best.

The Messiah is coming. He came once in humility, and He is coming again in glory. And the Church must be ready. Let us return to the altar. Let us offer Him more than ritual—let us offer Him ourselves.

Reflection

Have you ever offered God something less than your best? What led you there?

What does it mean to you that God desires pure worship, not performance?

How does Malachi's warning awaken your heart to prepare for Christ's return?

Prayer: Bring Me Back to the Altar

Righteous Father,
You are worthy of honor, awe, and holy sacrifice.
Forgive me for where I've brought casual offerings
to a holy table.
I don't want routine—I want revival.
I don't want comfort—I want communion.
Bring me back to the altar.
Burn away my complacency.
Light the fire again.

Let my worship rise with reverence,
and let my life reflect the glory of Your name.
The Messiah is coming.
Make me ready.
In Jesus' name, Amen.

Day 26 – The Table of Transformation

SCRIPTURE:

"³⁴The Son of man is come eating and drinking; and ye say, Behold a gluttonous man, and a winebibber, a friend of publicans and sinners!" Luke 7:34

"²And the Pharisees and scribes murmured, saying, This man receiveth sinners, and eateth with them." —Luke 15:2

Devotional Meditation

Jesus didn't just preach to sinners—He dined with them. In a culture where shared meals meant shared lives, this was radical love on display. The religious elite murmured, "He welcomes sinners and eats with them." They meant it as an insult. Heaven took it as a compliment. They didn't realize that restoration is found at His Table.

At Simon the Pharisee's table, a sinful woman wept at Jesus' feet. At Levi's table, tax collectors feasted with the Savior. In every instance, Jesus didn't recoil from brokenness—He reclined beside it. The table became redemption. It became radical identification.

These weren't meals of tolerance; they were meals of transformation.

At His table, shame met sanctification, failure found forgiveness. Distance became intimacy. Those unworthy were called sons and daughters. The fragrance of repentance always mingled with the aroma of bread and oil. Repentance turned her life around. His love changed her forever!

Even now, Jesus invites the unclean, the overlooked, and the ashamed to come—not to a place of scrutiny, but a place of welcome. His table is not reserved for the righteous—it's set for the hungry. And when sinners sit with Jesus, they don't leave the same. His grace changes everything at the Table!

Reflection

Have you ever felt too unworthy to sit at the Lord's table? What truth does today's Scripture speak to that fear?

What does it mean to you personally that Jesus dines with sinners?

Who in your life needs to know there's still a place at the table for them?

Prayer: The Welcome of Grace

Lord Jesus, Friend of Sinners,
     You saw me when I was far off,
and You drew near with kindness.
You sat where others would not sit.
You made space for the broken, the impure, the rejected.
And You welcomed me.
Thank You for inviting me to the table,
not because I was worthy, but because You are love.
Help me never to take that grace for granted.

Make my heart a place of welcome for others,
just as You welcomed me.
May every meal be a reminder of mercy,
and every table a chance for redemption.
In Your holy name, Amen.

Day 27 – Table of Abundance: Feeding the 5000

SCRIPTURE:

"^{11}And Jesus took the loaves; and when he had given thanks, he distributed to the disciples, and the disciples to them that were set down; and likewise of the fishes as much as they would." —John 6:11

Devotional Meditation

In the wilderness once again, a multitude gathered—not to see signs, but to hear the words of life. Jesus, moved with compassion, refused to send them away hungry. With five loaves and two fish, He took what was not enough and made it more than enough. From scarcity to abundance, His Table was more than enough.

This wasn't just a miracle of multiplication—it was a revelation. The Bread of Life was feeding His people, just as God had fed Israel with manna. But this time, the Bread wasn't falling from the sky—it was handed from His own hands.

John records that Jesus gave thanks, then distributed. Thanksgiving always precedes the miracle. And as the bread passed from hand to hand, something heavenly happened: the people were satisfied. Not only was there enough—there were twelve baskets left over. More than they began with. More than they ever imagined possible.

Jesus feeds us not only with provision, but with Himself. He satisfies the soul as well as the stomach. The table of God never runs out, never runs dry, and never turns anyone away. And it all begins when we offer what little we have, with gratitude. His grace will be more than you can imagine. Trust Him.

Reflection

Are there areas in your life where you feel like your resources are "not enough"?

How does Jesus' response to the crowd challenge your trust in His provision?

What would it look like to offer your "loaves and fish" today with thanksgiving?

Prayer: Bread in His Hands

Lord Jesus, our Bread of Life,
    You see the hunger in the crowd and the hunger in me.
You take what little I have and multiply it.
You feed multitudes through hands that give thanks.
Teach me to trust Your abundance.
Help me to give what I have—even when it feels small.
Take my offering and make it overflow.
Thank You that You still set tables in barren places.
You still satisfy hearts that are hungry for more.
Let me eat from Your hand today, and find my fullness in You.
In Jesus' name, Amen.

Day 28 – The Table of Remembrance: Covenant Renewal

SCRIPTURE:

"¹⁹And he took bread, and gave thanks, and brake it, and gave unto them, saying, This is my body which is given for you: this do in remembrance of me." —Luke 22:19

Devotional Meditation

The Table of the Lord is a place of remembrance—not of vague nostalgia, but of covenant clarity. When Jesus broke the bread and lifted the cup, He wasn't inviting the disciples into a sentimental ritual. He was establishing a living memorial of His sacrifice—a table where grace would meet them again and again.

"Do this in remembrance of Me" is more than memory—it is identity- sacred memory. We come to the Table not just to look back at the cross, but to remember who we are because of it. This meal renews the covenant in our hearts and reorients our lives around the One who gave Himself for us.

At this table, we are reminded of our forgiveness. We are reminded of His love. We are reminded that we belong—not because of what we've done, but because of what He has done. He took our place.

Every time we eat this bread and drink this cup, we are saying again, "I remember. I believe. I belong." And in that act, heaven touches earth. He is coming again.

Reflection

What does the word "remembrance" mean to you in the context of communion?

How does remembering Christ's sacrifice renew your faith today?

In what areas of your life do you need to remember who you are in Christ?

Prayer: Help Me Remember

Jesus,
    You gave everything for me—
and I never want to forget.
When the world distracts me,
when my heart grows cold,
when my thoughts drift from truth—
bring me back to Your table.
Help me to remember Your body broken,
Your blood poured out,
Your covenant sealed in love.
Let every communion be a fresh encounter.
Let every remembrance revive my heart.
I am Yours—today and forever.
In Your name, Amen.

Day 29 – Table of the Covenant: The Cup of Redemption

SCRIPTURE:

"¹⁹And he took bread, and gave thanks, and brake it, and gave unto them, saying, This is my body which is given for you: this do in remembrance of me. ²⁰Likewise also the cup after supper, saying, This cup is the new testament in my blood, which is shed for you" —Luke 22:19–20

Devotional Meditation

In an upper room, on the eve of betrayal, Jesus didn't raise a sword, not an army—He raised a cup. He broke bread, not to share a meal of celebration, but to begin a covenant of redemption. This was more than tradition. It was the fulfillment of every sacrifice, the embodiment of every promise. The table became an altar, and the meal became a memorial of eternal love.

Jesus held up the bread and said, "This is My body." Not a metaphor. Not mere symbol but substance. A declaration. "Given for you." His body, broken to make us whole. His blood poured out to make us holy. Love cleanses us and seals a covenant that never fades.

At that table, Judas was still present. The disciples still struggled. Peter would still deny. Yet Jesus served. He washed their feet. He offered the cup. He gave His body with full knowledge of their frailty. That's covenant love. It meets us in weakness, and yet never withdraws the invitation. The Table is still there.

This table is our table too. Every time we receive communion, we proclaim His death until He comes. We remember the cost. We receive His grace. And we recommit our hearts to the One who gave everything to bring us back to the Father's house. The Table connects us together- this cup makes us one!

Reflection

What does "this is My body, given for you" mean to your heart today?

Do you receive the cup of the new covenant with reverence, or has it become routine?

How does Christ's example of covenant love challenge the way you serve others?

Prayer: Covenant in the Cup

Blessed Jesus, Lamb of God,
     You gave Your body to be broken.
You poured out Your blood to make me clean.
And You welcomed me to a table I did not deserve.
Help me never to forget the cost of this covenant.
Let every cup I raise in remembrance be filled with reverence.
Let every piece of broken bread soften my heart again.
Make me a vessel of covenant love.
Let my life echo the words You spoke—

"Given for you."

In Jesus' name, Amen.

Day 30- The Table of Resurrection: Sweetness After the Tomb

SCRIPTURE:

"⁴²And they gave him a piece of a broiled fish, and of an honeycomb. ⁴³And he took it, and did eat before them." —Luke 24:42–43

Devotional Meditation

The tomb was empty. The stone was rolled away. And yet, the disciples still trembled in confusion and fear. Into that room, Jesus appeared—risen, glorified, and full of peace. And what did He ask for?

Something to eat.

They gave Him fish—and honeycomb. The room was ablaze with wonder. The disciples gaze on in awe.

In a moment that echoed eternity, Jesus—our risen Lord—took honey into His hands. Honey, not only a food of sweetness, but a symbol of delight, fulfillment, and divine promise. He who had tasted death now tasted sweetness. Not because He needed to be nourished—but because we needed to know:

The victory is real. The body is real. The resurrection is real.

He ate not because He was hungry, but because He was revealing something eternal. In that honeycomb was the sweetness of fulfilled prophecy. It was a reminder that life had triumphed over death. The Lion of the tribe of Judah had overcome. It was the intimacy and assurance of the Table.

The Table of Resurrection is the place where the impossible becomes personal. Jesus ate honey before them, not just to prove He was alive, but to invite them to taste and see. The bitterness of the cross gave way to the sweetness of the resurrection.

This table is for all who've walked through dark valleys, who've stared down the lion of despair or grief, and need to find honey in the hard places. He hasn't changed. He is still the same. Christ's resurrection offers more than hope for the future—it offers revival now. It calls us to live, not in fear, but in the light of His victory. The assurance of His Presence filled them with peace and the covenant of the Table still remains. Let His Table call you to assurance today. He rose in glory. He appeared in peace. And He asked for a meal. Not fancy. No frills. Just food, fellowship - and a table.

Honey after the grave means your story doesn't end in sorrow. There is sweetness waiting beyond the suffering.

The Lord Who walked out of the tomb brought peace, and He brought fellowship. This is Victory. This is life. Death isn't final.

When Jesus ate honey before His disciples, He was doing more than showing them He was alive. He was inviting them into a life where bitterness no longer has the final word. Hatred is gone forever. Failure has been swallowed in the grave. He restored faith, overflowing joy, and reminding them that even after death, God prepares a Table.

This is the table of new life. This is the sweetness after the tomb. The tomb isn't the end - it is the beginning. And it belongs to those who trust in Christ.

Reflection

Have you found spiritual honey even in places of sorrow or loss?

What does Jesus' choice to eat in His resurrected body reveal to you about His presence today?

How can you live with resurrection dedication and joy?

Prayer: Let Me Taste Resurrection

Risen Lord,
You triumphed over death.
You stepped out of the grave with fire in Your eyes
and honey in Your hand.
Feed me, Lord—
not just with knowledge, but with Your life.
Let the sweetness of resurrection fill my soul.
Let every place of defeat become a testimony of Your power.
Give me revival in the ruins.
Let me taste honey from the lion's mouth.
Let me walk in resurrection strength
and dedicate my life to You once again.
In Your name, the name that rose,
Amen.

Day 31 – Table of Recognition: Opened Eyes

SCRIPTURE:

"**30**And it came to pass, as he sat at meat with them, he took bread, and blessed it, and brake, and gave to them. **31**And their eyes were opened, and they knew him; and he vanished out of their sight...."
—Luke 24:30–31

Devotional Meditation

Two weary disciples walked the road to Emmaus, their hearts heavy with disappointment. The cross had crushed their hopes. The empty tomb had confused their faith. And though the risen Christ Himself walked beside them, they did not recognize Him.

But then—at the table, with bread in His hands—their eyes were opened.

It wasn't in the miracles, or the explanation of Scriptures, but in the breaking of bread that their grief turned to wonder.

This simple act of communion became the doorway to revelation. As the bread broke, their blindness lifted, and their hearts began to burn with holy fire.

The table is where Jesus still reveals Himself. It's in the ordinary—the breaking, the sharing, the giving—that He opens our eyes. When we come to the table weary, discouraged, or confused, He meets us not just to teach us, but to feed us. He breaks the bread—and in doing so, breaks open our understanding.

This isn't just about a physical meal. It's about spiritual awakening. Christ is revealed when we come close. And often, the table becomes the turning point from despair to destiny. This isn't ruin its revival. Repentance isn't the end - its relationship. This is where faith begins!

Reflection

Are there places in your life where you're walking in confusion or disappointment, like the Emmaus road?

How has Jesus revealed Himself to you in simple, unexpected moments?

What can you do to prepare your heart to meet Him in the breaking of bread?

Prayer: Open My Eyes, Lord

Lord Jesus,
You walk with me even when I don't recognize You.
You speak truth even when my heart is slow to believe.
And You break bread to open my eyes.
Today, I bring my questions, my discouragement, my silence.
Meet me at the table.
Let the bread speak what words cannot.
Let my heart burn again with love for You.
Thank You for the sacredness of the simple.
Thank You for revealing Yourself in the breaking of bread.

Open my eyes.
Make my heart aflame.
In Your name I pray, Amen.

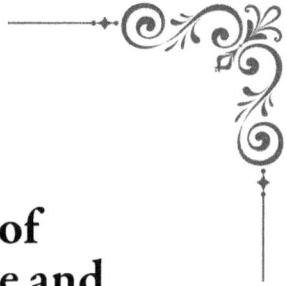

Day 32 - Table of Restoration: Come and Dine

SCRIPTURE:

"^{12}Jesus saith unto them, Come and dine. And none of the disciples durst ask him, Who art thou? knowing that it was the Lord. ^{13}Jesus then cometh, and taketh bread, and giveth them, and fish likewise." —John 21:12–13

Devotional Meditation

Jesus has risen. He sent them to Galilee. They went to the ship. They had returned to the nets. It was a memory – calling three years earlier. They followed Him - He is commissioning them again.

Jesus met them on the shore—not with rebuke, but with breakfast. The fire was already burning. The bread was already baking. And the risen Lord was already waiting.

This table was different from the Last Supper. That table looked ahead to suffering; this one looked back on it. That one prepared them for the cross; this one prepared them for restoration. This prepared them for Pentecost.

Peter, still carrying the weight of denial, found not condemnation, but invitation: "Come and dine."

Jesus didn't confront Peter with accusation—He restored him with questions. "Do you love Me?" This was the call of love to a heart that was hesitant. And with every answer, the fire burned brighter, not on the shore—but in Peter's heart.

This is the power of the resurrected Christ. He calls us not merely to believe in His victory but to dine in His grace. He prepares a meal where failure is met with mercy, where love is reawakened, and where peace is kindled around the warmth of fellowship. There the fire of Pentecost would spark. It was there that revival began. He is calling you today. Won't you come and dine?

Reflection

What is Jesus saying to you through the words, "Come and have breakfast"?

Is there any place of failure in your heart that needs the healing warmth of His restoration?

How does the presence of Jesus change the way you see your past and your future?

Prayer: Rekindled by Grace

Risen Lord,
You built a fire when I was cold.
You called to me when I went back to what I left behind.
And You prepared a table, even after my failure.
Thank You for not giving up on me.
Thank You for feeding me when I had nothing left.
Restore my heart again.
Ask me the hard questions.
And reignite my love for You.

I will come and dine.

I will eat what You have prepared.

And I will walk forward, restored and recommissioned, in Your grace.

In Jesus' name, Amen.

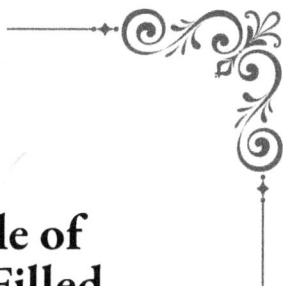

Day 33 - The Table of Pentecost: Spirit-Filled Fellowship

SCRIPTURE:

"⁴²And they continued stedfastly in the apostles' doctrine and fellowship, and in breaking of bread, and in prayers.." —Acts 2:42

Devotional Meditation

Pentecost wasn't just a moment—it became a movement. And at the heart of that movement was a table.

After the fire fell and the Spirit filled, the early Church gathered—not in temples alone, but in homes. Not around thrones of power, but around tables of communion. And what did they do? They broke bread. They prayed. They listened. They shared. And the presence of the Lord rested on them with power. This was healing, this was restoration, this was the taste of redemption. This was the heartbeat of God.

The outpouring of the Holy Spirit didn't distance the people—it drew them together. They didn't just have individual encounters with God; they became a family. And the table was their altar of unity.

This wasn't stale religion—it was burning love. They met daily with gladness. They gave sacrificially. And in that atmosphere of Spirit-filled fellowship, signs and wonders followed, the Church expanded, and joy overflowed. People were healed and needs were met.

To break bread together was to live in covenant together. Pentecost wasn't just tongues of fire—it was hearts on fire, drawn together in Christ. The Spirit descended—the Kingdom came - and a new kind of table was born: one of unity, holiness, joy, and supernatural growth.

Reflection

What role does the table—shared meals, communion, prayer—play in your walk with God today?

Are you cultivating fellowship that is Spirit-filled and devoted, or simply social?

How might the Lord be calling you to re-devote yourself to this rhythm of revival?

Prayer: Set the Table on Fire

Oh Lord,
        You fell like fire and filled the room.
You turned strangers into family,
and made the table a place of miracles.
Do it again in me.
Let my life burn with devotion.
Let my table be a place of covenant love.
Let my prayers be fueled by Your presence.
Unite us again, Lord—not just in belief, but in love.
Let our fellowship be more than social—it must be sacred.
And let the breaking of bread awaken Your power in our midst.
Set the table on fire.
In Jesus' name, Amen.

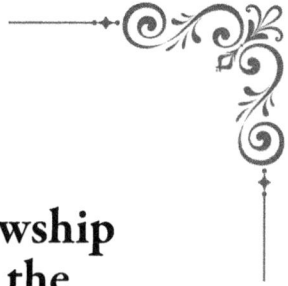

Day 34 – The Fellowship Table: United in the Spirit

SCRIPTURE:

"⁴⁶And they, continuing daily with one accord in the temple, and breaking bread from house to house, did eat their meat with gladness and singleness of heart," —Acts 2:46

Devotional Meditation

The early Church was marked by many things—apostolic preaching, signs and wonders, bold prayers—but woven through it all was this beautiful thread: fellowship. They broke bread not only in the temple but in each other's homes. At these simple tables, a holy unity was formed.

This was more than shared meals—it was shared lives. They shared His life - His life became theirs.

The Table of the Lord in the New Testament wasn't confined to sacred buildings. It was alive in living rooms and kitchens, where the Spirit of God knit hearts together in love. As they gathered, ate, and remembered Jesus, a supernatural bond grew. Walls came down. Needs were met. Joy overflowed.

The fellowship table reminds us that Christianity is not a solo journey. We are a people of covenant community. The Spirit not only draws us to Christ but to each other. And it is at the table—where bread is broken and hearts are open—that revival takes root in relationship.

Reflection

How has God used fellowship around the table to encourage and grow your faith?

Is there someone you could invite to your table to share life and Christ together?

What does it look like to cultivate community that is Spirit-filled and sincere?

Prayer: Make Us One

L ord of the Table,
      You draw us together with love stronger than fear,
with grace deeper than offense,
with joy greater than division.
Unite us, Holy Spirit.
Let our homes become altars of fellowship.
Let our meals become moments of ministry.
Let our hearts beat as one.
Make us one, as You are one.
And may the world see Jesus in our unity.
In Your name, Amen.

Day 35 – Table of Unity: Breaking the One Bread

SCRIPTURE:

"¹⁷For we being many are one bread, and one body: for we are all partakers of that one bread. " —1 Corinthians 10:17

Devotional Meditation

The table is not only a place of remembrance—it's a place of union. In the breaking of bread, the early Church didn't just remember Christ—they remembered each other. The same bread that symbolized His body reminded them that they were now His body on earth. As He is so they became.

Paul's words to the Corinthians cut through division: "We who are many are one body." They had turned the Lord's Supper into a fractured meal—some feasting, others going hungry. But Paul reminded them: You are one because He is one. You can become like Him too.

Every time we partake of the bread, we proclaim not only His death—but our unity. The body of Christ cannot be divided at the table. To break bread with others is to confess: I need you. We are in covenant together. We were saved by the same blood, filled by the same Spirit, and seated at the same table of grace.

This unity isn't fragile. It's forged in Christ's own body. The table becomes the altar where self-dies, pride surrenders, and love is rekindled. The fire will fall again!

Reflection

Do you see the Lord's Table as a call to deeper unity with other believers?

Are there any relationships in your spiritual community that need reconciliation before the table?

How can you contribute to the unity and love of Christ's body today?

Prayer: One Bread, One Body

Lord Jesus,
    You are the Bread of Life,
and You have made us one in You.
Help me to cherish the unity of the Spirit.
Remove every root of division from my heart.
Let love be my portion at the table.
Let humility rule over pride.
And let my hands be open to serve, not to strike.
Thank You that through Your broken body,
we have become one body—united, forgiven, and filled.
Make me an agent of Your peace,
and a keeper of the unity You purchased with blood.
In Jesus' name, Amen.

Day 36 - Discern the Body: A Call to Holy Communion

SCRIPTURE:

"²⁹For he that eateth and drinketh unworthily, eateth and drinketh damnation to himself, not discerning the Lord's body. ³⁰For this cause many are weak and sickly among you, and many sleep." —1 Corinthians 11:29–30

Devotional Meditation

There is a holy weight to the Lord's Table. It is not to be approached casually, carelessly, or with hidden offense. Paul warns the Corinthians that to partake without discerning the body brings consequences—weakness, sickness, and even premature death.

Why such strong words? Because the Table is not just about you and Jesus—it's about you and the Body of Christ. To discern the body means to recognize the sacredness of both Christ's sacrifice and His Church. Broken relationships, unrepented sin, prideful division—these defile the Table and block the flow of grace.

Communion is meant to heal, but when we come with hypocrisy or harboring division, it becomes a place of judgment instead of blessing.

To discern the body is to remember that the same blood that purchased your salvation purchased your brother's. The same grace that welcomes you welcomes them. The Lord's Table is not a throne for the perfect—it is a seat for the repentant, the humble, the reconciled.

No one looks the same at the Table. Seeing Christ in others makes all the difference. His Church is His Temple. When we examine ourselves rightly and walk in the light with one another, the Table becomes a fountain of healing, revival, and renewal.

Reflection

Are there any unresolved offenses or divisions in your heart before approaching the Lord's Table?

What does it mean to you to "discern the body"?

How can you prepare your heart in reverence and unity to receive communion rightly?

Prayer: A Heart that Discerns

Lord Jesus,
     Your body was broken for my wholeness.
Your blood was shed for my forgiveness.
And You've called me to walk in love with Your Body—the Church.
Search me, Lord.
Reveal any bitterness, pride, or hidden sin.
Give me grace to reconcile.
Give me humility to forgive and be forgiven.
May I never approach Your Table lightly.
Let me discern the body with holy fear and deep love.
And as I come, let it be for my healing, not my harm.

Cleanse me. Heal me. Unite me.
In Jesus' name, Amen.

Day 37 – Table of Unity: Breaking the One Bread

SCRIPTURE:

"[17]For we being many are one bread, and one body: for we are all partakers of that one bread." —1 Corinthians 10:17

Devotional Meditation

The table is not only a place of remembrance—it's a place of union. In the breaking of bread, the early Church didn't just remember Christ—they remembered each other. The same bread that symbolized His body reminded them that they were now His body on earth. As He is so they became.

Paul's words to the Corinthians cut through division: "We who are many are one body." They had turned the Lord's Supper into a fractured meal—some feasting, others going hungry. But Paul reminded them: You are one because He is one. You can become like Him too.

Every time we partake of the bread, we proclaim not only His death—but our unity. The body of Christ cannot be divided at the table. To break bread with others is to confess: I need you. We are in covenant together. We were saved by the same blood, filled by the same Spirit, and seated at the same table of grace.

This unity isn't fragile. It's forged in Christ's own body. The table becomes the altar where self dies, pride surrenders, and love is rekindled. The fire will fall again!

Reflection

Do you see the Lord's Table as a call to deeper unity with other believers?

Are there any relationships in your spiritual community that need reconciliation before the table?

How can you contribute to the unity and love of Christ's body today?

Prayer: One Bread, One Body

L ord Jesus,
   You are the Bread of Life,
and You have made us one in You.
Help me to cherish the unity of the Spirit.
Remove every root of division from my heart.
Let love be my portion at the table.
Let humility rule over pride.
And let my hands be open to serve, not to strike.
Thank You that through Your broken body,
we have become one body—united, forgiven, and filled.
Make me an agent of Your peace,
and a keeper of the unity You purchased with blood.
In Jesus' name, Amen.

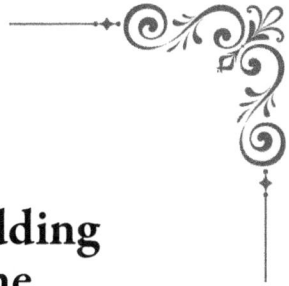

Day 38 – The Wedding Table: Everyone Welcome

SCRIPTURE:

"⁹And he saith unto me, Write, Blessed are they which are called unto the marriage supper of the Lamb. And he saith unto me, These are the true sayings of God." -Revelation 19:9

Devotional Meditation

From Genesis to Revelation, the story of God unfolds like a great feast. It began with fellowship in Eden, it was renewed at Sinai and sealed at Calvary—but it culminates in a wedding.

Heaven's final celebration is not a courtroom, a battlefield, or even a throne room—it is a table. And at this table, the Lamb is the Bridegroom, and the Church is His radiant Bride.

The Marriage Supper of the Lamb is the fulfillment of every longing. Every communion we've shared on earth is but a foretaste of this banquet. Every table of repentance, every altar of fire, every fellowship meal has pointed to this final day—when Jesus will wipe away every tear and host His beloved forever.

To be invited to this wedding table is the highest honor. But this invitation is not earned—it is given. And it is given to the meek, the washed, the ready. The Spirit and the Bride say, "Come!"

Your name is on the guest list. The table is being set. The celebration has no end.

Reflection

- • What does it mean to you to be invited to the Marriage Supper of the Lamb?

- • How does this future table give you hope in the present?

- • Are you living as one who is eagerly awaiting the Bridegroom?

Prayer: Prepare Me for the Wedding Feast

Bridegroom of Heaven,
      Thank You for inviting me.
Thank You for washing me clean,
for clothing me in Your righteousness,
and calling me Your own.
Prepare me for the wedding.
Keep my heart pure, my lamp burning,
my eyes fixed on You.
Let me live every day in the light of eternity.
Let me hunger for the joy of that final feast.
And let me never lose sight of the Bridegroom who comes in glory.
Even so, come, Lord Jesus.
Amen.

Day 39 – Heaven's Banquet Table

SCRIPTURE:

"⁹And he saith unto me, Write, Blessed are they which are called unto the marriage supper of the Lamb. And he saith unto me, These are the true sayings of God." Revelation 19:9

Devotional Meditation

At the culmination of history, when all tears are wiped away and every enemy is underfoot, there will be a feast. Not a battle cry—but a wedding song. Not a throne of judgment—but a table of joy. This is the Marriage Supper of the Lamb, the celebration of Christ and His Bride, the Church.

It is the table for which all other tables have pointed. The Passover foreshadowed it. The Last Supper prepared us for it. Every communion is a preview. And when this feast comes, it will be the final fulfillment—when the Lamb who was slain sits at the head of the table and His Bride is clothed in glory.

This is not a table of fear, but of union. Not a table of sorrow, but of celebration. And the invitation is still open: "Blessed are those who are invited." This blessing is not earned—it is received through grace. To sit at this table is to be loved with an everlasting love.

And even now, Jesus is preparing this feast. Heaven is setting the table.

And until that day, we gather at the Lord's Table with hope, saying, "Even so, come, Lord Jesus."

Reflection

• When you think of the Marriage Supper of the Lamb, what emotions or hopes stir in your heart?

• Are you living today as one who is preparing for that great banquet?

• How can each communion meal become a rehearsal for that eternal celebration?

Prayer: Come, Lord Jesus

O blessed Jesus,
You have loved me with an everlasting love.
You have clothed me in righteousness.
And You have invited me to dine at Your eternal table.
Thank You for the promise of the Marriage Supper.
Thank You for preparing a place for me.
Let my life be a song of readiness.
Let my heart burn with expectation.
Until that day, I will break bread in faith.
I will worship in hope.
And I will live in love.
Come quickly, Lord Jesus.
Come and receive Your Bride.
Amen.

Day 40 – The Eternal Table: No More Tears, Only Glory

SCRIPTURE:

"⁴And God shall wipe away all tears from their eyes; and there shall be no more death, neither sorrow, nor crying, neither shall there be any more pain: for the former things are passed away." —Revelation 21:4

Devotional Meditation

The journey ends not in sorrow, but in glory.

Every table we've visited in Scripture—every feast of covenant, every meal of mercy, every altar of fire—has led to this: the eternal table of the New Jerusalem. The story that began in a garden and passed through a wilderness, a cross, and a resurrection, finds its home in a city of light where God dwells with His people forever.

Here, there is no more separation. No more shame. No more tears.

This is the promise of the table prepared in eternity. It is not temporary nourishment—it is eternal communion. The Lamb who was slain now reigns. The Bride who was waiting is now adorned. The feast is no longer a rehearsal. It is the real thing.

As you close this 30-day journey, lift your eyes. Let your heart soar in the hope that all things will be made new. Every pain you've walked through, every tear you've cried, every table you've longed to sit at—it all finds its healing here.

You were made for this Table.

Reflection

How does the promise of the eternal table reshape your view of life's trials?

What does "no more tears" mean for you personally in this season?

How can you live today with your heart anchored in eternity?

Prayer: Home at the Table

Eternal God,
　　Thank You for the hope of heaven.
Thank You for preparing a place where sorrow dies,
and joy never ends.
I long for that day.
But while I wait, let my life be a foretaste—
a witness to Your goodness,
a vessel of Your love,
a table of Your grace for others to encounter.
Keep me faithful.
Keep me joyful.
And when the feast begins,
seat me near Your heart forever.
In Jesus' name, Amen.

Continued - No More Tears: The Final Table

SCRIPTURE:

"⁴And God shall wipe away all tears from their eyes; and there shall be no more death, neither sorrow, nor crying, neither shall there be any more pain: for the former things are passed away." —Revelation 21:4

Devotional Meditation

The story doesn't end in suffering—it ends in supper. It ends with a city, a table, and a God who wipes away every tear.

Heaven is not just a place of glory—it is a place of healing. The final table is not for the strong, but for those who have overcome by grace. It is set for those who have wept, struggled, longed, and persevered in faith. And when we finally sit at that table, God Himself will serve us joy.

There will be no more empty chairs from death. No more regrets. No more silent prayers unanswered. No more pain that lingers in the soul. At this final table, the old order of grief will give way to the eternal order of glory.

This promise is not just for the distant future—it is the anchor of our present hope. When we come to the Lord's Table now, we taste the bread and drink the cup knowing that one day, this temporary meal will be swallowed up in a forever communion. . And every tear we've cried on earth will be wiped away by the hand of the One who walked through death to be with us forever. Until sadness is swallowed by joy, until faith becomes sight. Our song is being written here, but in heaven the melody will be perfected. The story doesn't end in suffering—it ends in supper. It ends with a city, a table, and a God who wipes away every tear. Let Him wipe away yours today. Heaven is waiting – the Table is spread.

Reflection

What tears or burdens are you carrying that you long for God to wipe away?

How does the hope of the final table shape the way you live, grieve, or rejoice today?

Who around you needs to hear that there's a table of healing and restoration awaiting them?

Prayer: Wipe Away My Tears

Father of Mercy,
       You see my tears.
You know my pain.
And You promise a day when mourning will end.
Thank You for the hope of the final table.
Thank You that this life is not the end of the story.
Help me to live with eternity in view.
Let Your presence be my healing,
and Your promises be my strength.
Wipe away my sorrow with the cloth of heaven.
Restore my soul with joy that never fades.
And until I sit at that eternal table,
let my heart be filled with Your peace.

In Jesus' name, Amen.

Conclusion – Until He Comes: Living Between the Tables

SCRIPTURE:

"²⁶For as often as ye eat this bread, and drink this cup, ye do shew the Lord's death till he come." —1 Corinthians 11:26

Devotional Meditation

Every believer lives between two tables. The first is the Table of the Lord, set in the Upper Room, where Jesus broke the bread, lifted the cup, and gave Himself for us. The second is the Marriage Supper of the Lamb, the final banquet in heaven when all sorrow is gone and the redeemed are gathered home.

Between those two tables stretches the whole journey of the Christian life. Here, in this in-between space, is where we find ourselves—walking by faith, longing for glory, nourished by grace.

This is the tension of the "already" and the "not yet." Already redeemed but not yet resurrected. Already tasting, but not yet fully feasting. Already seated with Christ in heavenly places, but still living as pilgrims on earth.

And yet—it is in this space that God calls us to revival.

The Table as Memory and Mission

At the Lord's Table we remember. We remember His sacrifice. We remember His covenant. We remember that He has not left us as orphans, but comes to us in bread and cup, Spirit and Word.

But the Table is not only memory—it is mission. Paul says, "as often as ye eat... ye do shew the Lord's death." Every communion service is a sermon. Every table becomes a witness. The Church proclaims to the world: There is a Savior. There is forgiveness. There is covenant love.

Living between the tables means living as a people of proclamation. We don't merely consume—we declare.

The Table as Revival Fire

Revival doesn't always begin in stadiums or crusades—it often begins in kitchens, in prayer rooms, at humble tables where bread is broken and hearts are humbled.

When we discern the Lord's Body, we lay aside division and find unity. When we confess at the Table, we are cleansed afresh. When we eat in faith, the Spirit ignites passion.

The Lord's Table is not a ritual of religion but the rhythm of revival. Every loaf broken in love, every cup lifted in covenant, every gathering of believers who expect His presence becomes a place where heaven touches earth.

The Table as Presence and Peace

Jesus promised, "Lo, I am with you always." At the Table we experience that promise. His presence is not theoretical—it is tangible. In breaking the bread, our eyes are opened like the disciples at Emmaus. In lifting the cup, we taste the sweetness of fellowship restored.

And with His presence comes peace. Not the fragile peace of this world, but the wholeness of shalom—the peace of sins forgiven, the peace of reconciled relationships, the peace of hearts anchored in hope.

The Table as Anticipation

The final word is anticipation. Every meal here is a foretaste of the meal to come. Every communion is a rehearsal for the cosmic wedding feast. Every tear shed now is a reminder that one day there will be no more tears, no more death, no more sorrow.

This anticipation doesn't make us retreat from the world—it sends us into it. We live as people of hope, carrying the aroma of eternity, offering the invitation: "Blessed are those who are called to the marriage supper of the Lamb."

We live between two tables—the one in the Upper Room and the one in the New Jerusalem. One marked by a cross, the other by a crown. One soaked in sorrow, the other bursting with celebration. One promising redemption, the other fulfilling redemption. And in between, we are invited again and again to the Lord's Table, where memory meets hope.

When we eat the bread and drink the cup, we proclaim—not only what Christ has done, but what He will do. The Table is not just a backward glance; it is a forward leaning. Every communion is a declaration: "He is coming again."

We don't feast in finality—we feast in faith.

This world may groan with waiting, but the Table reminds us that Jesus keeps His promises. The same Lord who gave His body will return in glory. The same hands that broke bread will wipe away every tear. The Table grounds us in grace and lifts our eyes toward glory.

Until He comes. We live in unity. We love. We work.

So how shall we live between tables? With holiness. With joy. With expectation. Abiding in Revival. Living in hope. Loving with remembrance. Faithful in calling. We break the bread not just in remembrance, but in resolve—until He comes. The relationship is maintained, love stays kindled, repentance becomes our lifestyle. Revival becomes our life.

Living Between the Tables

So what does it mean for us?

◇ It means we repent often—for the Table demands a clean heart.

◇ It means we love deeply—for the Table unites us as one Body.

◇ It means we worship passionately—for the Table draws heaven near.

◇ It means we witness boldly—for the Table proclaims Christ until He comes.

◇ It means we hope expectantly—for the Table points us forward to glory.

We live between the tables. We linger in the tension. We proclaim in the meantime. We hunger for more.

And one day soon, the wait will be over.

Prayer: Until He Comes

Lord Jesus, Keeper of the Tables,
        We thank You for the cross and we long for the crown.

We bless You for the bread and the cup, and we hunger for the banquet still to come.

Help us to live faithfully in the space between—

not as wanderers without hope, but as children of covenant, a people marked by repentance, love, and revival.

Make our homes tables of presence.

Make our churches tables of fire.

Make our lives tables of welcome,

where sinners and saints alike can taste Your goodness.

And when the last trumpet sounds,

when the Bridegroom comes for His Bride,

may we be found ready—hearts burning, lamps filled, tables spread—

to sit down with You at the Marriage Supper of the Lamb.

Until then, Lord, we will keep coming.

We will keep proclaiming.

We will keep longing.

We will keep loving.

For we live between the tables—until You come.

Amen

Reflection

- How often do you think of the Lord's return when receiving communion?

- In what ways can the Lord's Table stir a fresh hope in your daily walk?

- What does it mean to live "between tables" in your relationships, worship, and mission?

Author's Note

GROWING UP IN THE HEART of the Appalachian Mountains, the table was more than just a place to eat—it was the center of our lives. Though each family member had their daily responsibilities—working construction, feeding livestock, going to school—one thing remained constant: we always came together at the table each evening. That table became a generational and cultural anchor.

My mother's grandparents, Grat and Chorilda Horton, had eleven children. Every evening, no matter what the day had held, they gathered at the table. There may not always have been abundance, but there was always togetherness. And there, they read Scripture, discussed the day, and kept faith alive.

In my own upbringing, the significant conversations that shaped who I became happened at the table. Raised in a Pastor's home, my parents, Gary M and Debra E. Roberts, lived out their ministry not just in the church, but around our family table. During revival meetings, church fellowship, or just simple family dinners, I remember discipleship moments that marked me for life. Around that table, we discussed doctrine, wrestled with Scripture, laughed, cried, and dreamed.

At my grandparent's home, Ralph and Doris Horton, the table was sacred ground. After Sunday school and the morning service, the family would gather to eat and talk—about the message, the past week, and the week ahead. Looking back now, having lived over 50 years, I realize that some of the most meaningful moments in my life happened around that table. Most of those family members are gone now, but their memory lives on through the lessons and love shared over those meals.

I can still name the preachers, the revivalists, the saints who sat at our table and poured into my life. Those conversations were discipleship. That laughter was fellowship. That time was holy.

My wife, Regina, and the Fuller family shared the exact same culture. The table has united us together for over 33 years. She grew up around the table—her family gathered the same way. After we were married, I came to understand the blessing of family gathering and how God shaped her life through it. Every single year in the Appalachian Mountains, their family reunions brought people from all over the United States to her family's table. It was called a family gathering—the Fuller family reunion time of celebration and remembrance. Over 35 years of this gathering, I've seen so many come and go, so many who have passed on but the gathering still happens and the table of reunion remains.

Every Christmas season, while gifts are exchanged, as time goes on we realize the Table becomes more important. The fellowship becomes more vital. The testimonies of good times, God's goodness, and joyful memories became the center of our celebration. People may come and go—times change, but the Table still stands.

The final Table has not yet been spread. There is another gathering coming. The Great Marriage Supper of the Lamb. Every meal of devotion, every Seder of remembrance, every Sabbath of rest, every sacred conversation is but a shadow of that glorious feast to come.

When we sit at our earthly tables and remember the Passover, or celebrate a simple meal in His Name, we are tasting eternity in advance. As the Israelites gathered around the table for the Shabbat meal each week to bless, reflect, renew and rest, our families need to remember the reason, reflect and rest in the assurance of the Table.

Let this book be an invitation for you—whether used as a devotional, a Bible study aid, or as a small group teaching guide—to return to the beauty and power of the table. I hope it inspires you to put away distractions, silence the technology, and be fully present. The conversations that take place around the table matter. They shape hearts. They disciple generations.

I thank God for the tables that formed me. All those who filled them with love, faith, and joy. He has a table prepared for us. I'm looking forward to the day when we are all gathered at His table, sharing blessings untold.

May we never lose sight of the wonder of the Lord's Table where love and fellowship abide forever. We have the sweet memory of all those who have passed on and together share in hope of what's still to come. You see - there is an Eternal Table that lasts where memories will never end, and it lies just ahead. He is the center of it. He has prepared it. Until that time, we can share His Word together and break the bread of the kingdom – where revival never ends.

Maranatha!

Aaron Roberts

References and Credits

USE OF SCRIPTURAL AND Historical Sources

All Scripture quotations are taken from the King James Version (KJV) of the Bible, which is in the public domain and free for commercial and non-commercial use without restriction.

Historical or theological references (e.g., Hebraic terms, early Church practices) are either in the public domain or used interpretively in a manner that reflects original synthesis and commentary, not reproduction of protected material.

Lexical and Theological Sources

• Strong, James. Strongs Exhaustive Concordance of the Bible. Public Domain. Definitions and original language for Hebrew and Greek terms

• Brown, Francis; Driver, S.R.; Briggs, Charles A. The Brown-Driver-Briggs Hebrew and English Lexicon. Public Domain

• R.A. Torrey, The Treasury of Scripture Knowledge, Public Domain.

Acknowledgements and Final Notes

This work draws richly from the inspiration of the Holy Scriptures and the leading of the Holy Spirit, with careful attention to historical, theological, and pastoral sources.

Gratitude is extended to the many voices in Church history and contemporary teaching who continue to guide the Church back to the Table—into revival, fellowship, and covenant love. All glory to the Lamb, Who was slain, and Who lives forevermore.

About the Author

AARON ROBERTS WAS BORN in the small town of Richlands, Virginia, nestled in the heart of the Appalachian Mountains. The son of Pastor Gary M. and Debra E. Roberts, Aaron grew up attending church where his father ministered faithfully until his passing in 2021.

What marked his life most profoundly were the revival messages followed by the altar services and the sacred meals shared afterward. In that small Appalachian church, the communion meal—the bread, the wine, the prayer, and the fellowship—deeply shaped his spiritual journey. His father's words echoing through the small church as he led the Lord's Supper – "As oft as you eat this bread and drink this cup ye to show the Lord's death - until He comes" left a lasting memory and inspired a holy reverence for communion and desire for revival. The awe of God's presence during those moments left an indelible mark on his heart.

Called to the ministry at a young age, Aaron's life and writing reflect a deep longing for revival, the fear of the Lord, and the table of communion that binds the Church in covenant love. He and his wife, Regina, have a shared passion to call God's people back to repentance, holiness, and the fire of the altar—to become once again a people for His love. Since 2009, through Victory Life - the Lord has moved in five countries in Africa to host small group bible schools training up leaders for the next generation. God has poured Himself out through these vessels- over 200 churches have been pioneered in Uganda, Africa alone, as the Lord moved through this ministry. This book supports their ministry as they spread the gospel of the Lord Jesus Christ.

Don't miss out!

Visit the website below and you can sign up to receive emails whenever Aaron Roberts publishes a new book. There's no charge and no obligation.

https://books2read.com/r/B-A-QXRGE-BFURG

BOOKS 2 READ

Connecting independent readers to independent writers.